P9-CRA-813

Discovering Great Jazz

"There are many books available on jazz. This one, I think, you'll find a bit different. *Discovering Great Jazz* began as a simple idea to present a straightforward, easy-to-read history of jazz as concisely as possible.

"Instead of esoteric analysis, there will be just enough to let the new listener know what to listen for. Instead of breaking jazz into big major periods, we will simply progress chronologically (with some overlap), telling without fuss what changes or developments were made. And when the time comes for recommending records, only those that best exemplify the era in question will be mentioned.

"This volume then can be considered both a refresher course for those who know what happened and an education for those who don't.

"I can at least promise this: Buying this book is cheaper than taking a jazz course."

—*Stephen M. Stroff,*
from the Introduction

A NEWMARKET DISCOVERING GREAT MUSIC SERIES BOOK

Discovering Great Jazz

*A New Listener's Guide to the Sounds and Styles
of the Top Musicians and Their Recordings
on CDs, LPs, and Cassettes*

STEPHEN M. STROFF

NEWMARKET PRESS
New York

Updated edition 1993

Copyright © 1991 by Stephen M. Stroff

This book is published simultaneously in
the United States of America and in Canada.

All rights reserved. This book may not be reproduced,
in whole or in part, in any form, without written permission. Inquiries
should be addressed to: Permissions Department, Newmarket Press,
18 East 48th Street, New York, N.Y. 10017.

93 94   10 9 8 7 6 5 4 3 2

Library of Congress Cataloging-in-Publication Data
Stroff, Stephen M.
Discovering great jazz : a new listener's guide to the sounds
and styles of the top musicians and their recordings on CDs, LPs,
and cassettes / Stephen M. Stroff.
p.   cm. — (A Newmarket discovering great music series book)
Includes bibliographical references and index.
ISBN 1–55704–169–5
1. Jazz—History and criticism.   2. Jazz—Discography.   I. Title.
II. Series.
ML3506.S89   1991
781.65'09—dc20   91–20285
                                       CIP
                                       MN

QUANTITY PURCHASES

Companies, professional groups, clubs, and other organizations may
qualify for special terms when ordering quantities of this title.
For information, write Special Sales, Newmarket Press,
18 East 48th Street, New York, N.Y. 10017,
or call (212) 832-3575.

Manufactured in the United States of America

To Diane, who works her tail off
so I can write books like this.

Contents

Preface

Discovering Great Jazz began as a simple idea to present a straightforward, easy-to-read history of jazz as concisely as possible. Having found no publisher, I initially ran off a hundred copies at my own expense. To my surprise, the copies sold out within six months. Clearly I had not counted on the public support of my efforts, the obvious need for such a book, and—most crucially—the encouragement and suggestion for an expanded edition from jazz critic Stanley Dance.

As a result, you hold in your hands a revised alter ego of the original version. Taking up Mr. Dance's suggestions, I have enlarged the sections on Earl Hines and Johnny Hodges, and included the great Bennie Moten big band. In addition, I have highlighted other musicians (Richard M. Jones, Cab Calloway, Glen Gray, Illinois Jacquet, Charlie Ventura, Errol Garner, Stan Getz, George Russell, Charles Mingus, Ramsey Lewis, Chick Corea, Rahsaan Roland Kirk, Cleo Laine, Al Jarreau, and Jack Walrath) who had been omitted from the original version. I have also incorporated into the text references to jazz on compact discs, which are becoming more and more common every year. (There still remains an appendix of jazz on compact discs that have not been mentioned in the text.)

On the other hand, I chose not to follow Mr. Dance's suggestion to eliminate references to out-of-print recordings. It's deplorable that the record companies refuse to keep many great recordings in print; and if a newly issued CD compilation drops some very important or irreplaceable recordings, it should be incumbent on the record company to republish the missing material. Almost every major city in this country has used-record shops and libraries where many of the albums I recommend can be found. Nevertheless, the recent slew of reissues (especially from RCA, God bless them!) has kept such listings to a minimum.

I hope and trust that my efforts to rectify the situations noted above are met with approval. Barring some wholesale changes in the jazz market, this new, improved version should stand up for years to come.

—STEPHEN M. STROFF

Introduction

There are many books available on jazz. Some go over its history in painstaking detail, often bringing the reader to the point of boredom before the message can be absorbed. Some analyze the music so much that enjoying the listening experience becomes secondary. Still others recommend hundreds of recordings, usually without rhyme or reason, apparently to show off the writer's knowledge without helping the neophyte.

This one, I think, you'll find a bit different.

Instead of esoteric analysis, there will be just enough to let the new listener know what to listen for. Instead of breaking jazz into big major periods, we will simply progress chronologically (with some overlap), telling without fuss what changes or developments were made. And when the time comes for recommending records, only those that best exemplify the era in question will be mentioned, since I doubt that most readers have Fort Knox at their disposal for purchases. Indeed, most of the discs recommended are budget issues or ones any good-sized library can be expected to have on hand, so checking out an individual artist (or any era) may require no more than eight dollars or your library card.

Obviously, then, this book is geared toward the new jazz

listener. Or is it? In a poll conducted among some five thousand "jazz fans" in 1985, less than 20 percent knew of any style or player who came up before 1960; less than 10 percent knew of any jazz prior to 1945; and less than 5 percent had ever listened to jazz recorded before 1935. This indicates a pretty sad and dangerous tendency, even for those who profess to know the music, to be ignorant of the past as if it didn't exist.

My own experiences as jazz editor of *Goldmine* tended to bear this out. Of the several jazz writers who contributed, only two had a working knowledge of many earlier players— and one of these was Ralph Berton, who lived through most of its history. By cutting themselves off from the Bunny Berigans, Jack Teagardens, and Jelly Roll Mortons of the music, the rest were only depriving themselves. Some beautiful and memorable music was permanently preserved in wax during those formative years, but they didn't seem to care. Since *Goldmine* was a historical record collectors' publication, the focus was as much on the old as the new; but when I asked one of my writers to do a piece on a "historical" figure, the first name that popped into his head was Freddie Hubbard!

This volume, then, can be considered both a refresher course for those who know what happened before 1950 and an education for those who don't. To my knowledge there is no book like this, so at the very least I feel I'm contributing to the general knowledge of Americans—who of all the jazz lovers in the world seem on average to least understand and appreciate our native musical art form.

I can at least promise this: Buying this book is cheaper than taking a jazz course.

Please note that the following abbreviations are used in the listings of the recordings: LP (long-playing record), CD (compact disc), Cs (cassette), OP (out of print), tks. (takes), and vers. (versions).

1.
Prehistory and Formative Years

Put as bluntly as possible, jazz developed because black musicians had inferior musical instruments.

You had to see it from their side. By the 1890s, they were a people all dressed up with no place to go—recently freed slaves (or their descendants) with limited employment possibilities, a by-product of the whites' subtle repression that included making a formal education virtually inaccessible. This is a social issue far too broad to discuss here in depth, but it is noteworthy that Scott Joplin, one of the great early ragtime composers (and a name that most people know nowadays), who was college-trained, based the plot of his ragtime opera *Treemonisha* on the necessity of gaining education as a means of freeing his fellow blacks from the shackles of folklore and superstition. Without repeating the error of the old stereotype that "all blacks have rhythm," it is nevertheless a fact that the various Negroid races who were forcibly transported to America enjoyed highly rhythmic music, something that was part and parcel of their African (or West Indian) heritage. Yet the music they played and sang in *this* country, especially after a few generations had passed, was not purely African or West Indian. It was an amalgam of gospel, chant, spiritual, minstrel, folk, and marching-band music.

Since they were poor, these early black musicians couldn't afford brand-new, well-made instruments like the whites, so they had to settle for beat-up, thirdhand trumpets and trombones. These instruments were sometimes incapable of being played in tune or even of playing certain notes at all. Thus the famed flatted thirds and fifths of jazz music were introduced, in part, because of the defects of the instruments. In addition, most of these musicians could not afford formal lessons, so they made it a basic rule in the early days to cultivate personal expression first and technique second. In some ways this might resemble trying to build a cathedral out of a Tinkertoy set. But that is exactly what they did: They built a cathedral of sound in a musical idiom that was related to, yet different from, the white culture that surrounded them.

The early influence of folk music—both the white variety as well as the Mexican, French, and West Indian varieties that flowed into their musical vocabulary—has led some observers to call jazz a form of folk music. But its development away from this sphere, even by as early as 1905, denies this argument. As trumpeter Harry "Sweets" Edison has said, "Jazz ain't folk music . . . it's too goddamned hard to play." Nevertheless, the folk influence is important; or, to be more precise, the manner in which black musicians turned folk music around to suit their own personal style was significant.

A superb example of such a performer was Huddie Ledbetter, better known as **Leadbelly** (1879–1949). He led a rough-and-tumble life, drinking and gambling; he once killed a man in a drunken brawl over disputed cheating at cards, and was sentenced to many years of hard labor in a federal penitentiary. As a result, Leadbelly was not a free man again until the 1930s.

In a strange sort of way, the punishment of his long incarceration was an ironic blessing to historians of jazz's early roots. By being cut off and taken out of the mainstream of developing jazz styles, Leadbelly retained the earlier, more primitive style that influenced the birth of the music. He played twelve-string guitar and a little piano, using both to accompany his blues- and work-song-drenched vocal style. The songs he performed, both originals and those learned by ear from others, were thus an odd mixture of traditional chording, flatted thirds, and funky renderings, primitive ragtime and traditional work songs and field chants. His 1944 recordings for Capitol Records can still be heard on Capitol CDP/C41B-92075 (CD/Cs); they include his own classics "Goodnight, Irene," "Rock Island Line," and "Ella Speed," piano folk music such as "Rock Eagle Rag," and folk "standards" such as "Take This Hammer" and "Tell Me, Baby"— all of which were "sanitized" by white performers during the folk music revival of the 1950s. Yet listening to Leadbelly's original performances, we hear an authentic rendering of the styles that influenced jazz, including the blues.

The blues were an offshoot of field chants, but whereas field chants, which were merely a series of repeated phrases, had no discernible form, the blues adopted a fairly standard twelve-bar length. The blues could also be quite melodic at times, often staying rather simple, although their primary purpose was to express longing, love lost, and personal pain. One of the greatest early blues singers was **Gertrude "Ma" Rainey** (1886–1939), who had been a star with the Rabbit Foot Minstrels at the turn of the century. Her voice was a rich contralto, her diction clear, and her style introspective: A superb example of her art, "Hear Me Talkin' to Ya," is available on both *Jazz Vol. 11* (Folkways FJ-2811, LP) and *Chicago* (BBC Records REB/CD/ZCF-589, LP/CD/Cs).

The other semi-"folk" music that influenced jazz was the jug or "spasm" bands that played out in the streets. These musicians were so poor they couldn't afford even fourthhand trumpets or clarinets, so they played anything that was handy: kazoos, ukuleles, cowbells, woodblocks, washtub basses, combs with tissue paper, cardboard boxes, whiskey jugs, and the inevitable washboard. Oddly, these groups retained their popularity well into the late 1920s, when the ruralization of certain sections of America was much more pronounced than it is today. This "low-down" influence migrated from Texas and Tennessee to Louisiana, and several examples still exist on record today. The album *Jazz Vol. 3: New Orleans* (Folkways FJ-2803, LP) features one such performance, "Bottle It Up and Go"; the late-'20s performance of "Memphis Shake" by the Dixieland Jug Blowers, on the album *Chicago* (BBC REB/CD/ZCF-589), includes the New Orleans clarinet of Johnny Dodds; and *The Immortal Jelly Roll Morton* (Milestone 2003, LP) contains similar performances of "Steady Roll" and "Mr. Jelly Lord." Indeed, the latter album is highly recommended for its odd mixture of pure jazz, folk music, and even slap-tongue vaudeville playing, all of which lend credence to Morton's later claims of the weirdly mixed styles that existed in New Orleans. The Caribbean influence and "Spanish tinge" is also felt in Morton's piano solo "Mamanita," which alternates between a straight 4/4 and tango rhythm, as well as in "New Orleans Joys" heard on *Jazz. Vol. 3*.

One of the biggest dance crazes of the 1890s, for both blacks and whites, was ragtime. Ragtime was march-tempo music that was highly syncopated. Its revival in our time has made it less of an antiquity. Like the marches themselves, rags followed a pretty strict formal structure of A melody, B melody, A repeated, then a C theme or "trio." The three most famous and popular ragtime composers were **Scott Joplin, Eubie Blake,** and **Joseph Lamb,** two blacks and a white man, respectively. This important development (like Leadbelly's transformations of folk and field music) was not jazz, but without it jazz probably would not have existed.

There are many ragtime recordings on the market: Some are all piano solos, some all band performances, a great many pseudo-ragtime played by people such as Jo Ann Castle, Mickie Finn, and Big Tiny Little—ricky-tick stuff on tack pianos in a style generally known as "honkytonk." Unfortunately, most of these are too slick to truly approximate the sound heard in New Orleans when the black musicians would "rag it," yet a few authentic recordings remain. On *Jazz Vol. 11: Addenda* (Folkways FJ-2811), Scott Joplin's piano roll of "Original Rags" may be heard; and on *Bunk Johnson: Last Testament* (CBS Special Products JCL-829, LP, OP), one of the true New Orleans originals leads his seven-piece band through Joplin's "The Entertainer" (erroneously attributed to J. R. Johnson on the label) and Albert Marshall's "Kinklets," more or less as they were heard in the early days. As for Eubie Blake, the out-of-print two-LP set *The Eighty-Six Years of Eubie Blake* (Columbia C2S-847) contains, in addition to a goodly amount of show tunes written by Blake and Noble Sissle in the 1920s, such valuable performances as Blake's ragtime transformation of "The Stars and Stripes Forever" and his original "Charleston Rag" (written nearly twenty years before James P. Johnson's more famous composition, "The Charleston").

The melding of ragtime piano music and the blues had a profound effect on the development of jazz, especially through the keyboard players. Sadly, few of the pioneers of jazz piano survive on recordings today, but in the playing of **Richard M. Jones** (1891–1945) one can hear the original New Orleans barrelhouse style, using several riffs and shifting the tonality from major to minor. One of Jones's few existing solos is the piano roll of "King of the Zulus Blues" on the album *Hot Jazz Piano Roll Hall of Fame* (Sandy Hook SH-2069, LP), with its rumbling, insistent bass patterns that undoubtedly influenced both the boogie and stride pianists of later generations. In addition, the same album features the only known solo by **Steve J. Lewis**, "Mama's Gone Goodbye." Surprisingly, this latter selection reveals a piano style even more sophisticated and complex than Jelly Roll Morton's; indeed, the constantly moving bass line and rolling, right-hand triplets sound eerily like early recordings of Earl Hines. Lewis's only claim to fame in later years was that he had toured with the band of A. J. Piron, but Richard M. Jones wrote the classic eight-bar blues "Trouble in Mind" and the blues-jazz standard "Tin Roof Blues" (originally "Jazzin' Babies Blues"). In addition, as recording director for OKeh in 1925, Jones initiated and produced the marathon record- ing sessions by Louis Armstrong's Hot Five and Hot Seven.

As for marches, which were heard in the streets of New Orleans during festivals and funerals, these were played by many bands, including the Eagle Band and the Superior Band. The leader of the Eagle was the man credited as the first great jazz musician, trumpeter **Charles "Buddy" Bolden** (1868–1931). A barber by day, Bolden went berserk during a street parade in 1907 and was committed to a mental in- stitution, where he died twenty-four years later; as a result, he never recorded. According to the best reports, we would today consider Bolden's style much closer to ragtime than jazz. The man who inherited his mantle as king, **Freddie Keppard** (1883–1932), did record in the 1920s and showed little swing or originality. Bolden's tone was powerful, how- ever, and he exerted a positive influence on others to take up horns and compete with him. One of the most famous of these was **Joseph "King" Oliver**, who will be discussed in more detail later.

When Bolden went insane in 1907, the Eagle Band was taken over by trombonist **Frankie Dusen**; in 1911 Bolden's former second trumpeter, **Willie "Bunk" Johnson** (1879– 1949), rejoined and became the new leader. Johnson's tone even then was considered somewhat weaker but much sweeter than Bolden's. In the 1940s, though past his prime, Johnson made some recordings of authentic early marching music that still exert a fascination today. Two examples are on the LP *Jazz Vol. 3: New Orleans* (Folkways FJ-2803): "Didn't He Ramble," the kind of tune the bands played coming back from a funeral, and "Down By the River," a spiritual.

New Orleans, where all these elements somehow came to- gether, was a curiously prejudiced town. Creoles were people of mixed French, Caribbean, and Spanish or Portuguese blood. Because they were not racially "pure" and spoke a pidgin language that was neither French nor Spanish, they were considered of a lower caste than white Anglo-Saxons. Some Creole men married "lower-class" white women, but most felt themselves drawn to blacks; as a result, there were some white Creoles, but the majority of Creoles were mulatto. Conversely, because of their French and Spanish background, black Creoles considered themselves superior to "Negroes" and only occasionally socialized with them. Whites *never* associated with blacks but sometimes talked to Creoles (white and mulatto); while octoroons, who had one-eighth black ancestry, were shunned by whites and blacks alike. The one place they condescended to meet one another was on the bandstand. Thus the Creoles learned some musical tricks from both sides and passed them along. In this crazy, roundabout way, all three races were included early on in the formation of jazz: the classical formality of traditional white music, the French and Spanish tinge, and the wild abandon and soul of the blacks.

In 1896, New Orleans alderman Sidney Story pushed an ordinance through the city council that restricted prostitution to a thirty-eight-block red-light district adjoining Canal Street. The area, nicknamed "Storyville," soon attracted the best ragtime pianists to play in the "houses," where they were called "professors." As time went on and as the music evolved, the pianists "jazzed up" the rags and eventually played original compositions. Bands also played in these "houses," as well as in the dance halls, where the usual instrumentation was the traditional New Orleans "front line," consisting of a trumpet, a trombone, and a clarinet. Soprano or alto saxophones were optional instruments, either as substitutions for or additions to the clarinet. In the whorehouses and dancehalls, the piano became part of the band, which had been impossible when playing music on the street.

But what exactly is the difference between ragtime and

jazz, and when did the change take place? Both questions are tricky to answer, since many early jazzers—Bolden, Keppard, Oliver, and even Johnson—stuck so close to the melody that calling their music jazz instead of ragtime is debatable. Generally, however, jazz is the improvisation of a new or countermelody on the chord changes of a certain song. In the beginning these improvisations were very rhythmic—sometimes consisting of no more than a few notes repeated over and over. This was eventually called a "riff." It came from the repeated chanting in black churches, a tradition that continues to this day. A little later, probably with the emergence of Oliver and Johnson, the rhythmic pattern would be varied every couple of bars or so. But true jazz, as we know and understand it today, took daring turns of improvisation that often resulted in an entirely new composition based on the chords of the original tune. Eventually, by the late 1930s, jazz musicians began substituting alternate chords in the underlying structure of the song as they improvised on the melody and rhythm, thus creating something quite complex while still retaining the trappings of popular music.

The most important traceable link between ragtime and jazz was the previously mentioned **Ferdinand "Jelly Roll" Morton** (1885–1941), though he leaned more toward jazz. A pianist who played in the Storyville bawdyhouses, nevertheless he did not develop a crude, "honky-tonk" style like that of Big Tiny Little's, but a curiously refined, structurally cohesive, harmonically (and rhythmically) adventurous style of jazz piano. He was jazz's first great composer—his productivity seems incredible today, especially considering the fact that most of his pieces follow the standard A-B-A-C structure of marches and ragtime. The subtle but important difference was that Jelly *swung*, which is to say that he accented his syncopations much more strongly than Joplin. He also introduced rhythmic and melodic improvisations on his own repeats of themes, instead of playing them over, note for note.

As a mulatto Creole, Morton was taught the usual prejudices. His condescension to black musicians didn't exactly earn him their love and respect. On the other hand, his compositions were so catchy that most blacks played them anyway, not to mention the whites, so that he remains an important early influence. Four of his earliest classics—*New Orleans Joys* (1902), *King Porter Stomp* (1905), *Grandpa's Spells* (c. 1908), and *The Pearls* (1918)—may all be heard on the album *Jelly Roll Morton, 1923–24* (Milestone MCD-47018-2, CD).

For a superb and fairly authentic example of how the early jazz bands sounded when they played for dancing, one need look no farther than Bunk Johnson. The following album also shows how the musicians transformed the (sung) blues tradition into genuine jazz music:

> *Bunk Johnson: The King of the Blues*/C.C. Rider (two vers.); Low Down Blues; St. Louis Blues; Blue as I Can Be; Dippermouth Blues; Midnight Blues; Weary Blues; New Iberia Blues; Careless Love; How Long Blues; Royal Garden Blues; and Tishomingo Blues. American Music AMCD-1 (available from Collector's Record Club, 1206 Decatur St., New Orleans, LA 70116).

Although these recordings were made in 1944 (Johnson never recorded before the 1940s), the musical approach is that of pre-1920 New Orleans. Indeed, the lineup of clarinetist George Lewis, trombonist Jim Robinson, bassist Alcide "Slow Drag" Pavageau, and drummer Warren "Baby" Dodds is entirely authentic; Lewis and Robinson later formed the nucleus of the Preservation Hall Jazz Band, which carried the old tradition into the 1970s. The sound quality is somewhat "bottomless," with the banjo, bass, and drums underrecorded, but the front line is clear and enticing. Note particularly how Johnson's lead weaves in and out of the ensemble, often playing the melody straight through with tremendous swing, using improvisation frugally but with telling effect. Even King Oliver considered Johnson his master in the blues; Bunk was unquestionably the most underrated of the early jazzmen, but history is all too often unfair to the real stylists.

The poor whites also played rags and marches, and when the innovations of Morton and Johnson made the music swing, the white musicians adopted those, too. At the same time that Bolden's Eagle Band played in the streets and dancehalls, so did the bands led by drummer **Jack "Papa" Laine** (1873–1959) and his sons. One of the younger generation of white musicians, and a Laine protégé, was cornetist **Nick La Rocca** (1885–1961), who in 1908 formed the Original Dixieland Jass Band (ODJB). "Jass" was the original spelling of the music, a term with distinctly sexual connotations. Such a latecomer could hardly be termed "original," but that was the name La Rocca gave his group, and in 1917—now spelling it with two *z*'s—they gained the distinction of being the first jazz band on records.

The story is encrusted in legend, hearsay, and braggadocio, often having emanated from Nick La Rocca himself, but here are the details as far as they are known. In 1916 Freddie Keppard was invited by Victor to make test pressings. He did so, but the acoustic system of recording—playing or singing directly into a long metal horn that engraved a limited range of sound directly onto a wax master—was fraught with dangers, the worst of which was that sudden loud noises knocked the stylus out of the groove. Because jazz is an alternation of soft and loud, that's just what happened, and on playback, Keppard's powerful tone kept wearing out the test pressings after just two plays (not a good record, even in those days of two-pound tone arms), so they were shelved and not issued.

In that same year, the ODJB arrived at the Casino Gardens in Chicago. After a stay there and at the Belvidere Hotel, they moved on to New York to play in Max Hart's Reisenweber Café on Columbus Circle. Despite stories by La Rocca to the contrary, the band wasn't an immediate success. Indeed, for the first two nights the patrons, scared out of their wits, sat on their hands and refused to approach the dance floor. On the third night, Max Hart himself got up and announced, "This music is for dancing." Finally one couple came unstuck, then another; they improvised some steps, and before long the ODJB (and Reisenweber's) were a smash hit. Al Jolson came to see them, as did Enrico Caruso and Paul Whiteman. Soon enough, the band was invited to record.

This time, in January 1917, it was Columbia that took the initiative, but Columbia—lacking faith in the commercial appeal of the band's "cacophony"—shelved the records and refused to issue them (though they did, eventually). Whatever possessed conservative Victor to rush in in February where Columbia feared to tread is anybody's guess, but that's exactly what staid Calvin Childs, Victor's A&R man, did. This time he put his best engineers on the sound problem. They eventually reduced Tony Sbarbaro's drum kit to bass drum and woodblocks, and put them and La Rocca's cornet in the back of the room facing away from the horn, but came up with two acceptable masters: "Livery Stable Blues" and "Dixieland Jazz Band One-Step," issued in March 1917 on Victor 18255. Jazz was finally on the market.

This story is told in detail not because the ODJB was such a superb band, but because they were so important historically. Had this attempt failed, it might have been years before any record company dared try anything like it again. On the other hand, the success of Victor 18255 allowed such standards of the early repertoire as "Lazy Daddy," "Fidgety Feet," "Ostrich Walk," "At the Jazz Band Ball," "Skeleton Jangle," and their biggest and most influential hit, "Tiger Rag," to come out on subsequent releases. Indeed, it even prompted timid Columbia to issue their ODJB record in April, but too late: The band was already established in the public mind with Victor. The best of the ODJB's early records are available on the following CD:

Sensation!/Livery Stable Blues; Dixie Jazz Band One-Step; Lazy Daddy; Bluin' the Blues; Fidgety Feet; Sensation Rag; Clarinet Marmalade; At the Jazz Band Ball; Look at

'Em Doin' It; Satanic Blues; Ostrich Walk; 'Lasses Candy; and five others. Living Era AJA/CDAJA-5023 (LP/CD, British).

Listening to them today, we hear more ragging than swinging, more hokum than heat, more vaudeville than sincerity. Yet in their time they were considered a great band. As to the question of what constitutes "swinging," this is actually more difficult than defining jazz itself.

In the best definition I can muster, "swinging" is taking the rhythmic value of any given note to its extreme breaking point before release. Take a quarter note, for instance. In ragtime and syncopated classical music, the accents would be marked by following that quarter note, played in strict time, with an eighth note and another quarter note *out* of strict time. To highlight the syncopation, the accompaniment might follow the opposite pattern—two eighth notes followed by a quarter note—thus giving an impression of constant counterpoint. In swinging a quarter note, all the work is up to the soloist, since the accompaniment might keep a strict 4/4 tempo behind him. Thus that same quarter note, when swung, might actually jump the beat by a fraction of a second, be held its full value, and then be released. It's something that almost has to be heard, since musical notation—after four centuries of development—never did catch up with the inflections of jazz. To this day, swinging cannot be properly notated.

A crude attempt at swinging was made by another famous early orchestra, King Oliver's Creole Jazz Band, which appeared at Chicago's Lincoln Gardens between 1921 and 1923. During its heyday, the band consisted of not the usual five but seven musicians: trombonist Honore Dutrey, clarinetist Johnny Dodds, pianist Lil Hardin, banjoist Bill Johnson, drummer Warren "Baby" Dodds, and two cornetists, Oliver and young Louis Armstrong. It was undoubtedly the presence of two major jazz names, Dodds and Armstrong, that has lent such an aura of mystique and attributed greatness to a mediocre outfit. But it must be remembered that Armstrong had not yet broken out of the New Orleans marching band/ragtime influence (as Jelly Roll Morton already had) to produce something unique and truly swinging; that didn't happen until late 1924 when, as featured soloist with Fletcher Henderson's big band, he was able to spread his wings and really fly.

Three examples of the Oliver group are on *Jazz Vol. 3*: "Snake Rag," "High Society," and "Dippermouth Blues." The first of these is a typical jazz-rag of the era, with a lot of fast action and syncopation, but little if any variations in a jazz sense. The section work shows the trick Oliver and Armstrong had worked out: They'd play with each other in thirds, Armstrong following Oliver's lead a fraction of a beat behind him. This simple but effective device gave the illusion of swinging, but it was an illusion only. In "Dippermouth," Dodds and Oliver take solos so famous that they would be copied as if etched in stone forevermore. In his solo, Oliver does swing a little, smearing notes and lifting the rhythm away from the beat, but the variations he plays are purely rhythmic and not beyond a five-note range.

The real hero of the Creole Jazz Band was clarinetist **Johnny Dodds** (1892–1940), who was, after Morton and Bunk Johnson, one of the finest early jazzers. His playing was fluid and mobile, with little of the stiffness one hears in the work of Keppard, La Rocca, and Oliver. We will run across Dodds again, in recordings by some Morton and Armstrong groups, but the following album—though featuring recordings made later than the early '20s—gives an accurate feel for early New Orleans polyphony as practiced by one of the original masters. Indeed, Dodds's acrid tone, affecting vibrato, and interesting configurations remained a jazz standard for years:

Johnny Dodds/Clarinet Wobble; Bucktown Stomp; Sobbin' Blues; If You Want to Be My Sugar Papa; Perdido Street Blues; Ballin' the Jack; Wild Man Blues; Idle Hour Special;

I Can't Say; Bull Fiddle Blues; Indigo Stomp; Grandma's Ball; Hen Party Blues; Wolverine Blues; San; and Forty and Tight. BBC REB/CD/ZCF-603 (LP/CD/Cs).

The above album contains another Creole Jazz Band tune ("Sobbin' Blues"), and two by Morton ("Wild Man" and "Wolverine"), yet the titles made under his own name and Jimmy Bertrand's Washboard Wizards come the closest to authentic small-group jazz, New Orleans-style. Characteristically, these late-'20s discs are rare because they didn't sell very well. By the latter part of the decade, Dodds's style was considered old-fashioned.

A year before the first Creole Jazz Band recordings, in 1922, a quite different New Orleans group made records in the Gennett Studios. This was the New Orleans Rhythm Kings, or NORK; and chronologically *their* clarinetist, **Leon Rappolo** (1902–1943), has the distinction of being the first bona fide jazz soloist on disc.

Before getting into the great and unique style played by Rappolo and the band, however, let's dispense with some of the misguided charges hurled at the NORK by several jazz "experts." First, they were attacked for "copying" Oliver's Creole Jazz Band—especially because they were an all-white outfit. But of the various players, only George Brunies's trombone syncopations even remotely resemble any of the Creole Jazz Band players', and Brunies's solos were far better constructed than Dutrey's. Jack Pettis's alto sax takes the role of contrapuntalist assigned to clarinet in the ODJB and Creole Jazz Band. And though Paul Mares (a white Creole) often played trumpet with a mute, he used a plunger with a "growl" rather than the straight cup mute Oliver fancied. As for Rappolo, his conception of the jazz solo was—for 1922—far ahead of its time.

The other charge laid against the NORK was "rhythmic sluggishness," especially in their recording of "Tin Roof Blues" (this was first levied against them by Rudi Blesh in the late 1940s, then seconded by Brian Rust in the 1950s). But the difference between what they claimed to hear and what is actually heard is probably attributed to their expectations. Because "Tin Roof Blues" was issued in 1923, they obviously expected to hear the typically excitable, foursquare approach exemplified by the ODJB or Creole Jazz Band, not the wonderfully relaxed atmosphere set and sustained by Mel Stitzel's fluid, flowing piano. Except for the surface crackle and sonic limitations, this record—especially in takes 1 and 3—sounds like a modern slow-blues performance. Nothing of the sort can be said for any of the records King Oliver ever made, with or without his often overrated band.

In July 1923, Jelly Roll Morton sat in for a handful of sides, including marvelous versions of his own compositions "Mr. Jelly Lord," "Milenberg Joys," and "London Blues." "Milenberg Joys" is reproduced on *Jazz Vol. 3*, along with Rappolo's pacesetting solo in "Tiger Rag" (*sans* Morton, Folkways FJ-2803). But the Rhythm Kings were so innovative and enjoyable, not to mention historically important, that the following collection—though somewhat muddy and muffled-sounding as a result of noise limiters—is highly recommended as the beginning of any well-balanced jazz library:

> *New Orleans Rhythm Kings*/Eccentric; Farewell Blues; Discontented Blues; Bugle Call Rag; Panama; Tiger Rag; Livery Stable Blues; Oriental; Sweet Lovin' Man; That's A-Plenty; Shimmeshawabble; Weary Blues; That Da Da Strain; Wolverine Blues; Maple Leaf Rag; Tin Roof Blues; Sobbin' Blues; Marguerite; Angry; Clarinet Marmalade (2 tks); Mr. Jelly Lord (2 tks); London Blues; Milenberg Joys (2 tks); and Mad. Milestone MCD-47020-2 (CD).

In all this material, one is constantly aware of an old style being made to sound fresh and new—despite the fact that these records were contemporaries of the ODJB and Creole Jazz Band sides that sound so corny today! In "Eccentric," for instance, the very first number they recorded, the somewhat vaudevillian effects of Pettis's alto sax are decidedly offset by the overall blend and flow of the band. In fact, *flow* is the key word here: For once, we are not so much aware of crunching rhythm or square corners in the swing, but an overall blend that moves, smoothly and inevitably, from first note to last. Mares's growling trumpet surpasses Oliver's in accent and control, but the real surprise comes from Rappolo's clarinet breaks. They shimmer with color, swing from one end of his range to the other unexpectedly, and provide the first example on record of the "pregnant pause"—a full bar's silence in one of them—before slurring up to an offbeat syncopated figure.

Compare, for instance, their already mentioned recording of "Tiger Rag" with the ODJB original. On the Victor, Larry Shields's clarinet provides the only real moments of traditional New Orleans playing, as a polyphonic (or counterpoint) instrument. Rappolo, on the other hand, is freed from that duty by virtue of Pettis's alto sax. As a result, he can take a full-chorus solo of unusual structure, actually creating a new melody over the chord changes of the original tune. And, unlike Oliver's solo in "Dippermouth Blues," Rappolo's on "Tiger Rag" is melodic and rhythmic, thus taking him to the front rank of jazz players in this still formative period. When Rappolo went insane in 1925, jazz lost a major voice and unsung giant.

Small wonder, then, that the NORK in general and Rappolo in particular had such a great influence on the young, white Chicago-area musicians. Among these were Joe Sullivan (piano), Jimmy MacPartland (cornet), Benny Goodman (clarinet, and the first to extend Rappolo's style on his own instrument), Muggsy Spanier (cornet/trumpet), Gene Krupa (drums), Bud Freeman (tenor sax), and especially the first great cornet soloist of the period, Bix Beiderbecke. But we'll save him to start the next chapter.

2.
Groundbreakers
of the Twenties

One "problem" that many buffs cannot overcome in respect to early jazz, and indeed all jazz up through the end of World War II, is the fact that a great deal of it was designed for dancing. This entertainment aspect, in their opinion, interfered with the creative side. While it is true that the number of "pure" jazz records made during this period are few and far between, in comparison to those made primarily for the dancing and (later) jukebox markets, such critics are undoubtedly not seeing the forest for the trees. The basic vocabulary of jazz, which is to say its harmonic-rhythmic language, was invented and honed from 1924 to 1945; whatever came after was merely an extension of the language and its several dialects developed in the midst of "entertaining."

In this respect, 1924 was an interesting year for jazz. The ODJB, having broken up and begun to fade from memory, was "saluted" in Aeolian Hall, New York (a venue then considered as prestigious as Carnegie), as "the wild, untamed beginnings of jazz" by popular bandleader Paul Whiteman. The previous year, Fletcher Henderson had formed an all-black popular dance band that slowly but surely worked its way toward jazz greatness. In late 1924 and early 1925, his trumpet section featured Louis Armstrong, who was working toward a new and unique style. Jean Goldkette, a French émigré, started a band that year in hopes of competing with Whiteman, but the band eventually reached a jazz level similar to Henderson's. Jelly Roll Morton was between contracts, having been shunted by Gennett but not yet signed by Paramount or Victor.

In February 1924 the Gennett label recorded a new sensation: a band of young, white college students (and dropouts), none of whom had ever seen New Orleans, called the Wolverines. As a whole, the Wolverines were a pretty poor group; unlike the Creole Jazz Band, they couldn't even hold a steady tempo sometimes. Trombonist Al Gandee played a stiff version of New Orleans "tailgate" style, and clarinetist Jimmy Hartwell, though trying to emulate Leon Rappolo, came off a poor second. What made them unique, and eventually remembered in jazz history, was the fact that they were Bix Beiderbecke's first band.

Leon Bix Beiderbecke (1903–1931)—the original jazz legend—was a cornetist who lived hard, died young, drank an awful lot of bad liquor along the way, and left in his wake a legacy of irreplaceable recordings. Whole chapters and books have been written about his magnificent, groundbreaking style, so I won't go into too much detail here. Besides, to modify the old adage, one recording is worth a thousand words.

Put as simply as possible, Bix Beiderbecke represented a whole new school of jazz playing at a time when the old still had another decade to run on its lease. Instead of pushing the rhythm incessantly, à la Keppard, La Rocca, and Oliver, Beiderbecke rode on it gracefully, almost coolly, using chromatics at a time when others were still figuring their way around a basic scale. There was some Rappolo in his playing—in fact, he was more influenced by the clarinetist than by any contemporary brass player—but also some Debussy and Ravel; Beiderbecke was the first jazz musician to incorporate modern classical elements in his playing. But that

doesn't mean he couldn't swing. Indeed, the archetypal Beiderbecke chorus began with a pretty, florid statement, logically constructed and impeccably played, followed by a
searing high-note blast, upward rip, or funky outburst that
would both summarize his previous statements and take the
listener by surprise. Small wonder, then, that a small-potatoes
band like the Wolverines could not contain his career. Even
in the limited opportunities of the 1920s, Beiderbecke made
it big. He spent two stints each with the Goldkette and Whiteman bands, considered the crème de la crème of popular
music.

Between 1924 and 1930 he recorded prolifically for a number of labels: Gennett, Victor, OKeh, Columbia, Harmony,
Pathé, and Brunswick all did well by his talent. But Bix was
haunted by the shadow of his family, who ostracized him for
being a jazzman instead of a "legit" symphony player, and
the conflict drove him farther into the wells of drink and
despair. When he died of lobar pneumonia in 1931, his life,
creative powers, and reputation were all on the wane. Beiderbecke's last months on earth were not pretty ones.

The inner struggle and bittersweet quality of his life are
all reflected in his pure, crystalline tone, undeniably the most
beautiful on records. Not surprisingly, the musicians he influenced directly—young, white Chicagoans who worshiped
him as a god—felt he represented the epitome of Dixieland
cornet, modern-style, which is to say with less ensemble polyphony and more solo room. Hearing him today, though,
one feels a closer kinship to later players such as Rex Stewart,
Miles Davis, and Chet Baker than to white Dixielanders such
as Jimmy MacPartland, who replaced him in the Wolverines.
The following albums contain Beiderbecke's finest work:

Singin' the Blues/Trumbology; Clarinet Marmalade; Singin'
the Blues; Ostrich Walk; Riverboat Shuffle; I'm Comin',
Virginia; Way Down Yonder in New Orleans; For No
Reason at All in C; Three Blind Mice; Blue River; There's
a Cradle in Caroline (two tks.); There Ain't No Land Like

Dixieland; In a Mist; Humpty Dumpty; Krazy Kat; Baltimore; Wringin' and Twistin'; Just an Hour of Love; and
I'm Wondering Who. CBS CK/CT-45450 (CD/Cs).

Bix Beiderbecke/At the Jazz Band Ball; Copenhagen; Royal
Garden Blues; Mississippi Mud; Sorry; Take Your To-
morrow; Rhythm King; Goose Pimples; Wa-Da-Da; Since
My Best Gal Turned Me Down; Deep Harlem; There'll
Come a Time; Barnacle Bill the Sailor; Rockin' Chair; I
Like That; and Jazz Me Blues. BBC REB/CD/ZCF-601 (LP/
CD/Cs).

The first album contains small-band recordings made during his second tenure with Goldkette, under the nominal
leadership of **Frank Trumbauer** (1900–1959), an interesting
C-melody sax player who acted like a "foster father" to Beiderbecke. Trumbauer's playing, liquid and relaxed, influenced sax players from Johnny Hodges to Lester Young.
Sometimes, as in "Trumbology," Beiderbecke's playing
tended toward mere virtuosity, replete with double and
triple-tonguing; more often, as in "Way Down Yonder" and
"Three Blind Mice," it had a fluid and subtly swinging approach. This compilation also features Beiderbecke's only
piano solo recording, the famous "In a Mist," with its De-
bussy-like use of passing chords and ambiguous tonality, combined with some genuine swinging. In the second album are
the best of those Chicago-Dixieland sides, made under the
name of Bix and His Gang. The lead work is particularly
confident, with the strong, exceptional standouts of "Jazz Me
Blues," "Goose Pimples," "Sorry," and "Since My Best Gal
Turned Me Down." Also included are cuts with the full
Whiteman band ("Mississippi Mud") as well as the studio
orchestras of Trumbauer, Irving Mills, and Hoagy Carmichael. "Copenhagen" is a better-than-average example of the
Wolverines.

Unfortunately, though some of the white musicians Beiderbecke influenced were quite fine, as a whole they pursued
a style largely dead-ended by its own limitations. Twenty
years hence they were still playing the same sort of loose

Dixie style represented on those records. The spiritual ring-leader of this particular group was banjoist/guitarist **Eddie Condon** (1905–1981). In the early 1940s, Condon organized concerts for his small but faithful band of followers who, like Peter Pan, refused to grow up. Since they played mostly at a club called Nick's, their music was dubbed "Nicksieland jazz"—a sadly apropos description for a style already becoming quite dated. Goodman, Krupa, and drummer Dave Tough were exceptions to this rule, and both Freeman and trumpeter Max Kaminsky were briefly a part of the big-band era, but most of the others had little or no effect on the evolving mainstream. One such performer whose career was unfortunately caught crosswise in time was **Francis "Muggsy" Spanier** (1906–1966).

Spanier, like Beiderbecke, was an enthusiastic youngster when jazz first came to Chicago in the early 1920s. Unlike Beiderbecke, however, he was not so much influenced by the work of Rappolo and the legendary (though unrecorded) cornetist Emmett Hardy as he was by the harder-swinging Paul Mares and Armstrong. Indeed, Spanier's style was an extension of Mares's and offered an alternative to Beiderbecke's as another white version of the black idiom. Spanier began recording at the young age of eighteen on six titles with a group called the Bucktown Five. He recorded two more a year later with the Stomp Six and then went on to years of big-band work with the pop bands of Ray Miller, Ted Lewis, and Ben Pollack. As a result, Spanier, widely acknowledged as one of the finest all-round lead cornets in the Chicago style, never got to show his true mettle until he organized his Ragtime Band in 1939.

This group, which included former NORK trombonist George Brunies and fellow Chicagoans clarinetist Rod Cless, guitarist Bob Casey, and drummer Don Carter, opened in the Windy City to such enthusiastic receptions that RCA gave them an immediate recording contract with their Bluebird label. Four sides were cut in Chicago, then twelve more when the band moved to Nick's in New York. They never got another booking beyond that point, for reasons never properly explained, yet these sixteen sides have been in print on and off for fifty years:

> *At the Jazz Band Ball*/Big Butter and Egg Man; Eccentric; That Da Da Strain; Someday Sweetheart; At the Jazz Band Ball; I Wish I Could Shimmy Like Sister Kate; Dippermouth Blues; Livery Stable Blues; Relaxin' at the Touro; Riverboat Shuffle; At Sundown; Bluin' the Blues; Lonesome Road; Dinah; Black and Blue; Mandy Make Up Your Mind. Plus two selections by Eddie Condon and four by Bud Freeman. RCA Bluebird 6752-2-RB (CD).

The group's playing is, in many ways, typical Chicago style: fast and loose, with integrated New Orleans polyphony alternated with lusty solo work. What makes Spanier's recordings so special, however, is their *joie de vivre* and the way each of the principals plays off the others. There is never a feeling of one-upmanship here, but instead a sense of "feeding lines" back and forth in a constant whirl of activity that makes the final result sound fuller and more orchestrated than normally expected from a septet basically playing head arrangements. (For comparison, listen to the Condon and Freeman sides, with their great soloists—Teagarden, Kaminsky, and Pee Wee Russell—but lack of cohesion.) If it is possible for a single set of records to truly represent a style, Spanier's clearly illustrates the white Chicago style.

In the meantime, while Beiderbecke was making jazz history with Goldkette, Whiteman, and the Bix and His Gang/ Frank Trumbauer sessions, **Louis Armstrong** (1901–1971) was doing something spectacular with Fletcher "Smack" Henderson, Erskine Tate, and his own Hot Five/Hot Seven. As Ralph Berton so aptly put it, it was like suddenly being switched from AC to DC current; certainly that's the effect of the Henderson cuts, where his then-stodgy band is galvanized by the power and drive of Armstrong's trumpet. Duke Ellington put it thus: "When Smack's orchestra began playing in the city with Louis, nobody had ever heard anything like it, and the impact cannot be put into words."

Like Beiderbecke, Armstrong's style developed over the years; unlike Beiderbecke, Armstrong's evolutions seemed to come in great leaps and bounds rather than gradually. No one who knew Armstrong just from his Creole Jazz Band recordings would ever suspect the driving powerhouse of the Henderson selections. Those who acclimated themselves to the Henderson cuts would then be surprised by the bold, wild rhythmic attacks of his 1926 and 1927 Hot Fives and Hot Sevens. And then, when it seemed there could be little more to add to his musical vocabulary, along came pianist **Earl Hines** (1905–1983) to spur him on to even greater heights. Armstrong would eventually reach a peak, from 1936 to 1942, that very few trumpeters would ever surpass— but now we're getting ahead of ourselves.

There's an early example of post-Oliver Armstrong on *Jazz Vol. 3*, "Cakewalking Babies From Home" with Sidney Bechet, Charlie Irvis, Lil Hardin, and Alberta Hunter. Then, on side 1 of the same LP, is "Keyhole Blues," by one of the Hot Sevens. By comparing these two selections, made only two and a half years apart, one can hear the tremendous growth of Louis as a soloist. In the latter recording, the steely brilliance of his sound and wonderful abandon of his swing practically leave his bandmates behind.

But that's just the tip of the iceberg. To truly appreciate the fullness of this era, one must hear the following albums:

Louis Armstrong 1: Young Louis/Words; When You Do What You Do; Lucy Long; Static Strut; Stomp Off, Let's Go; Georgia Bo Bo; I Ain't Gonna Play No Second Fiddle; Drop That Sack; Easy Come, Easy Go Blues; Blues Stampede; I'm Goin' Huntin'; If You Wanna Be My Sugar Papa; Weary Blues; Melancholy; New Orleans Stomp; and Wild Man Blues. MCA/MCAC-1301 (LP/Cs).

Louis Armstrong/Wild Man Blues; Snake Rag; Muskrat Ramble; Melancholy Blues; Willie the Weeper; Ory's Creole Trombone; Hotter Than That; Struttin' With Some Barbecue; Symphonic Raps; West End Blues; Muggles;

Save It, Pretty Mama; St. James Infirmary; Knockin' a Jug; and St. Louis Blues. BBC Records REB/CD/ZCF-597 (LP/CD/Cs).

These two albums cover a much wider range of material than the more common Columbia series. The MCA LP covers the Henderson band (first two selections), Perry Bradford's Jazz Phools, Erskine Tate's Vendôme Theatre Orchestra, Jimmy Bertrand's Washboard Wizards, and the Hot Five and Seven under pseudonyms. Indeed, this version of "Wild Man Blues" is actually superior to the Hot Seven version on Columbia, which begins the second album. Nonetheless, the BBC album contains such great Hot Five numbers as "Struttin' With Some Barbecue" and "Hotter Than That," as well as classic collaborations with Earl Hines, such as "Symphonic Raps," "Save It, Pretty Mama," "West End Blues," and "Muggles."

Those last two titles were also recorded under the name of the Hot Five, but notice how much more sophisticated and together this band sounds when compared to the earlier selections. It is true that any band with Earl Hines and without Lil "Stone Hands" Hardin could not help but improve, but Jimmy Strong's less old-fashioned clarinet makes a better foil for Armstrong's then-radical ideas than Dodds's. (Some writers feel that Dodds, who played well with Oliver and Morton, simply "froze" when Armstrong suddenly explored new directions.) The real gems here are "St. James Infirmary," "Save It, Pretty Mama," and especially "West End Blues." Armstrong tried to remake the last tune a few times in his career, but finally realized that what he'd done back in 1928 was unique and largely unsurpassable. Incidentally, the four quarter notes that open the record, strongly accented but played strictly in time, force a footnote to my definition of "swing."

Hines's piano style, emphasizing a florid, free-style right hand against a stabbing, jabbing left, was a unique departure from the locked-hands style of the ragtime and New Orleans pianists. Heard here in an embryonic stage, he reached his maturity in the mid-1930s recordings ("Angry," "Maple Leaf Rag," "Rosetta," and "Cavernism") with his excellent Grand Terrace orchestra (*South Side Swing*, MCA/MCAC-1311, LP/Cs). Hines's harmonic daring and freedom from cliché eventually influenced a new generation of pianists in the late 1940s, but again we get ahead of ourselves. Concurrent with his duties opposite Armstrong, he played at Chicago's Apex Club with New Orleans clarinetist **Jimmie Noone** (1895–1944), the most technically adept of the Crescent City reed players. Indeed, it was claimed that French composer Maurice Ravel once notated a solo by Noone, but was told by the first clarinetist of a symphony orchestra that parts of it were impossible to play!

Noone began on guitar, but by age fifteen was studying with Lorenzo Tio, the greatest of New Orleans clarinet teachers. Unlike his contemporary Dodds, Noone developed a sweet, liquid, even sensuous tone. In fact, it was claimed he didn't use a brass team in his Apex Club band so his sweet sound would not be overpowered (although in at least one session he did use cornetist George Mitchell, and trombonist Fayette Williams was a regular). In company with Hines and the obscure but excellent alto saxist Joe Poston, Noone explored the facets of his art that made him a legend (as well as an influence on Benny Goodman): the fluent, well-practiced runs, the elegant phrasing, and the occasional unexpected break, as heard below:

> *Oh! Sister, Ain't That Hot?*/Tight Like That; San; Love Me or Leave Me; My Daddy Rocks Me; El Rado Scuffle; Apex Blues No. 2; Chicago Rhythm; So Sweet; You Rascal You; Oh! Sister, Ain't That Hot? MCA/MCAC-1363 (LP/Cs).

The style bridging the gap between Jelly Roll Morton and Earl Hines was called "stride," and was immediately influential. Stride was a style in which the left hand, though basically a timekeeper, alternated strong, "walking" bass notes with triad chords while the right improvised freely. Left-hand octave jumps were frequently used as well. Hines, though initially influenced by stride, broke from its mold by avoiding constant chording and by playing the left hand closer to mid-keyboard.

James P. Johnson (1894–1955) is the man generally credited with inventing stride piano. Born in New Brunswick, New Jersey, he was (like Beiderbecke) intrigued by the classics. In fact, he received training in classical harmony and composition, which helped him develop his then unparalleled touch and technique. Like Morton, he was a prolific composer who started by expanding ragtime. His most famous tune, "Charleston," became a landmark for even pseudojazz bands in the 1920s. By 1923, however, his style evolved to the point where aspiring pianists literally came from miles around to pick up some pointers. Among these were Duke Ellington, Willie "The Lion" Smith, and Thomas "Fats" Waller.

Johnson's piano can be heard accompanying blues singers and with other jazz artists, but his solos remain the purest source of style. There are four superb ones on GRP/Decca Jazz GRD-604 (CD): "Cryin' for the Carolines," "You've Got to Be Modernistic," "Jingles," and "What Is This Thing Called Love." The first and last are reworkings of standard "pop" material. The third, while ostensibly a rag in form, is taken at a furious pace and swung mightily. "Modernistic," another original, is replete with unexpected musical gags, highly inventive riffs chasing each other to a furious conclusion. These four selections should be listened to more than once to fully appreciate the complexities developed on several levels. In every way, they are masterpieces.

During this decade the blues were reaching a high point and had a strong impact on the developing forms of jazz. Among the most famous practitioners were crude rural artists such as Blind Lemon Jefferson and Bukka White, yet it was the more sophisticated, pop-oriented style of the women blues artists that exerted the greatest influence in the jazz world. Among the most famous of these were Mamie Smith, Victoria Spivey, and the previously mentioned Gertrude "Ma" Rainey.

It was Ma Rainey's protégée **Bessie Smith** (1898–1937) who represents the pinnacle of the form, and, indeed, the era of classic blues is dated from her first records (1923) to her last (1933). Fortunately, the discs bear out her greatness in abundance. Bessie Smith possessed an alto voice fully as rich as Rainey's, but with an even more forceful projection and wider range of material. Bessie Smith was certainly not without flaws, and not all her records are equally good, but the selections on the following albums certainly give credence to her title as the "Empress of the Blues":

Bessie Smith/Empty Bed Blues; Alexander's Ragtime Band; At the Christmas Ball; Preachin' the Blues; Keep It to Yourself; He's Got Me Goin'; Trombone Cholly; Kitchen Man; You've Got to Give Me Some; Thinking Blues; Devil's Gonna Git You; Send Me to the 'Lectric Chair; Baby Doll; Take Me for a Buggy Ride; and Young Woman's Blues. BBC Records REB/CD/ZCF-602 (LP/CD/Cs).

Bessie Smith: The Collection/Downhearted Blues; Weepin' Willow Blues; 'Tain't Nobody's Bizness If I Do; My Sweetie Went Away; St. Louis Blues; Reckless Blues; You've Been a Good Ole Wagon; I Ain't Gonna Play No Second Fiddle; Young Woman's Blues; Mean Old Bedbug Blues; Muddy Water; Empty Bed Blues; Black Mountain Blues; Nobody Knows You When You're Down and Out; Gimme a Pigfoot; and Do Your Duty. CBS CJ/CK/CJT-44441 (LP/CD/Cs).

Some indication of her greatness is reflected in the fact that the best jazzmen of the era practically fought to work with her. On the recordings above, one can find such luminaries as pianists Clarence Williams and Fletcher Henderson, trumpeters Joe Smith and Louis Armstrong, trombonists Charlie Green and Jack Teagarden, clarinetists Benny Goodman and Buster Bailey, and drummer Kaiser Marshall. Each title yields its own pleasure, but "St. Louis Blues," "Second Fiddle," "Empty Bed Blues," "Downhearted Blues," "Nobody Knows You When You're Down and Out," "Alexander's Ragtime Band," and "Gimme a Pigfoot" are particularly fine. Fickle fate decreed that, during her lifetime, for the most part only blacks knew of her existence, while today many of her biggest fans are middle-class whites. Listeners today may be embarrassed by the rural-racist overtones of some of the lyrics, but the unashamedly emotional appeal of her singing and the power of her records haven't faded with time.

In 1926, Jelly Roll Morton returned to the recording studios. This may have meant little or nothing historically—after all, Morton had been one of the very early pioneers and had already made his mark on jazz—but musically, the best was yet to come. In addition to making the superb piano solos noted earlier, Morton crystallized his concept of band performance in a series of records for Victor under the moniker the Red Hot Peppers. At the time, the records were ridiculed by more forward-looking jazzmen as anachronisms, but with the passage of time we can hear them for what they are: thoughtfully composed, skillfully orchestrated, and mightily swinging vignettes of idealized New Orleans style, as seen through the mind of a musical genius. Traditional bands have come and gone since the Red Hot Peppers last entered a recording studio in 1930, but none has had the creativity or richness of detail found in the music of Morton's group.

Two brilliant (but isolated) examples are on the compendiums already mentioned: "Mournful Serenade" on *Jazz Vol. 3* and "Wild Man Blues" on *Johnny Dodds*. For greater variety in form and substance, however, the following album is highly recommended:

The Pearls/Black Bottom Stomp; Sidewalk Blues; The Chant; Dead Man Blues; Smokehouse Blues; Steamboat Stomp; Doctor Jazz; Original Jelly Roll Blues; Grandpa's

Spells; The Pearls; Cannonball Blues; Wolverine Blues;
Mr. Jelly Lord; Shreveport Stomp; Georgia Swing; Kansas
City Stomps; Deep Creek; Mournful Serenade; Red Hot
Pepper Stomp; Freakish; Buddy Bolden Blues; Tank
Town Bump; and Winin' Boy Blues. RCA Bluebird 6588-
1/2/4-RB (LP/CD/Cs).

The incredible variety of Morton's approaches to music,
both in orchestration and style, is absolutely amazing. One
will notice, for instance, his use of clarinet trios ("Sidewalk
Blues"), the alternation between brass and reeds ("The
Pearls"), and the colorful way in which tuba and drums are
used to accent the proceedings rather than bog them down.
At their best, Morton's band recordings are compositions in
which the parts—solo and ensemble—all combine to glorify
the whole. Indeed, their unity is such that after hearing them
a few times it becomes impossible to imagine any other *solo*
spots that could complement the *written* parts so well.

This leads, naturally, to the question, Is something this
thoroughly composed really jazz? The answer is yes. As we'll
see, the improvisations of a jazz musician aren't necessarily
or always made up on the spot—note Armstrong's "Wild Man
Blues," Bobby Hackett's "String of Pearls," Art Tatum's "Yesterdays," or any trumpet solo recorded by Sy Oliver. As long
as a solo is different from the original music and it swings,
it's jazz—despite what others may tell you!

Thus the Red Hot Peppers' recordings mark the end of
an era, but with an elegant and masterful flourish. Those
who prefer traditional or "Dixieland" groups should listen
closely to these sides; they may find their idols rather tar-
nished or strained beside the luminous beauty of Morton's
music. For, more than anything else, Morton was a colorist,
a genius at using just the right instrument at the right time,
for just the right effect. In that regard he was the predecessor
of Duke Ellington, and it is indeed ironic that neither man
had much use for the other.

While Morton was etching his legacy, the orchestra led by

Fletcher "Smack" Henderson (1898–1952) was developing rapidly as a major jazz ensemble. When Armstrong was in the trumpet section, they were—in a jazz sense—a rather mediocre band. But after Armstrong left, Henderson and chief arranger **Don Redman** (1900–1964) hit on a way to simulate Armstrong's power by having the whole trumpet section play a scored improvisation. Redman then scored similar playing for the reeds and had the two opposing sounds play off each other, in call-and-response, much like the praying in black churches. By using a driving rhythm section and modern Harlem-piano chords, the Henderson band was soon second to none. The following collection aptly sums up its musical history:

> *Fletcher Henderson: Building an American Orchestra*/The Gouge of Armour Ave.; Dicty Blues; Go 'Long, Mule; Shanghai Shuffle; Copenhagen; Naughty Man; TNT; The Stampede; Henderson Stomp; Snag It; Rocky Mountain Blues; Tozo; Wabash Blues; I'm Comin', Virginia; Whiteman Stomp; Hop Off; Blazin'; Somebody Loves Me; King Porter Stomp (three vers.); Keep a Song in Your Soul; Sugar Foot Stomp; Hot and Anxious; Honeysuckle Rose; Yeah, Man; Queer Notions; Can You Take It; Christopher Columbus; Stealin' Apples; Blue Lou; and Sing You Sinners. Smithsonian Coll. P2-13710 (two LPs).

Many selections, such as those on the last side, date from a later period than the 1920s and should be postponed listening for the time being. Nevertheless, traversing the first two sides in particular will illustrate the rapid growth of Henderson's band. The additions of Joe Smith and Tommy Ladnier in the trumpet section and especially of **Jimmy Harrison** (1900–1931) in the trombones helped moved Henderson's band into the forefront.

Harrison represented a major step forward in trombone playing. As was noted, the function of the instrument in New Orleans ensemble was basically counterpoint; its solos were usually heavy and leaden. George Brunies (of the NORK) and Miff Mole developed a staccato style that helped make its contributions a little more lithe. But with Harrison, we move toward a smoother, burnished, more "classical" sound, with a flowing legato and rather daring harmonics. From this point on, the trombone would be the equal of the clarinet and trumpet. It remains a great pity that Harrison, tied up contractually to Henderson, did not record during the 1920s with Armstrong.

For nearly a year, no one on record came close to Jimmy Harrison, though rumors flew about a young Texan who blew away everyone except Beiderbecke when he played with them. In 1928, in New York, rumor became reality when the young trombonist subbed for Miff Mole on a Roger Wolfe Kahn big-band date. This was **Weldon "Jack" Teagarden** (1905–1964), who revolutionized the instrument and for a decade remained its most eloquent exponent.

Because Teagarden learned the trombone as a child, when he had very short arms, he invented a series of false, close-to-the-shoulder slide positions where he could "lip" the notes into place. This is a complex and confusing way for anyone trained conventionally, but since Teagarden was used to it, it became second nature to him. Blessed with perfect pitch and a faultless ear—it was said he could "tell the overtones of a thunderclap"—Teagarden evolved a style using unusual leaps, rapid-fire triplets, and a marvelous sense of construction. Even more unusual, he was a first-rate jazz/blues singer, the first white man to equal Armstrong in this capacity, and thus could jam with both races without fear of inferiority.

Of the following two albums, the first covers more historic sessions; the second duplicates three titles (though only one identical recording) and is in electronic stereo, but it should be sought to appreciate the effect his playing had on early groups:

> *I Gotta Right to Sing the Blues*/I'm Gonna Stomp Mr. Henry Lee; That's a Serious Thing; Dinah; Never Had a Reason to Believe in You; Tailspin Blues; Sheik of Araby; Basin Street Blues; Beale Street Blues; Two Tickets to Georgia;

You Rascal You; I Gotta Right to Sing the Blues; Ain'tcha Glad?; Texas Tea Party; Dancing With Tears in My Eyes; A Hundred Years From Today; Fare Thee Well to Harlem; Christmas Night in Harlem; and Davenport Blues. Living Era/ASV AJA/CDAJA-5059 (LP/CD).

B. G. & Big Tea in NYC/Dinah; On the Alamo; Peg O' My Heart; Sweet Georgia Brown; China Boy; The Sheik of Araby; Keep a Song in Your Soul; Loved One (2 tks); Deep Harlem; Strut, Miss Lizzie; Beale Street Blues; After You've Gone; Farewell Blues; Someday, Sweetheart; It Had to be You; Sugar; Davenport Blues; Somebody Loves Me; and Riverboat Shuffle. GRP/Decca GRD-609 (CD).

On the first album, "Tailspin Blues" demands attention because of a unique trick that Teagarden invented. He would take the bell off the trombone and play with just the slide and water glass—thus eliminating any reference point for slide positions. (Most trombonists use the bell to judge where the slide goes to play certain notes.) On the second, we hear some marvelous recordings with Red Nichols (particularly "Indiana," "Sheik of Araby," and "Keep a Song in Your Soul"), arranged brilliantly by Glenn Miller.

In context with Teagarden, we should mention at this time two musicians who literally pioneered their instruments in jazz: violinist **Joe Venuti** (1904–1982) and guitarist **Eddie Lang** (1904–1933). The former took a vigorous, wildly swinging approach to his instrument unequaled until the arrival of Stuff Smith in the 1930s; and the latter was, undisputably, the most influential guitarist of his time. Lang's sense of rhythm was so impeccable and buoyant that drummers and bassists occasionally lagged behind him, and his single-note breaks gave a whole new dimension to the guitar as a solo instrument. This potential was later explored more fully by Dick McDonough and Charlie Christian, but only one man surpassed Lang as an all-around guitarist, and that was Django Reinhardt. Indeed, Lang was personally responsible for the guitar's ascension over the banjo in jazz bands. The following album showcases their contributions to the jazz vocabulary:

Joe Venuti–Eddie Lang/Stringing the Blues; Bugle Call Rag; Four String Joe; Krazy Kat; Sensation; My Baby Came Home; The Wild Dog; Church Street Sobbin' Blues; Shivery Stomp; Running Ragged; Hot Heels; Put and Take; Oh! Peter; Beale Street Blues; Vibraphonia; and Eddie's Twister. BBC Records REB/CD/ZCF-644 (LP/CD/Cs).

It's worthy to note here the innovative music of the Five Pennies, a recording-only group that experimented with substitute harmonics and swinging off the beat in a way that curiously presaged the bop era. In fact, their "cool" approach to jazz was decidedly off the beaten track for its time, and one for which they were heavily criticized.

The leader of this group, **Loring "Red" Nichols** (1905–1965), was derided before and after this period (1926–1932) as being no more than "a poor man's Bix Beiderbecke" (Ralph Berton), and indeed his usual style of cornet playing was pure but somewhat stilted in comparison with Beiderbecke's. Yet in these records under his own name, in conjunction with clarinetist/saxist **Jimmy Dorsey** (1904–1957), pianist **Arthur Schutt** (1902–1965), trombonist **Milfred "Miff" Mole** (1898–1961), guitarist Lang, and drummer **Vic Berton** (1896–1951), who had originally assembled the group and had coined the name Five Pennies, Nichols created a style that explored various ways of altering the beat and alternating tightly arranged passages with virtuosic solos:

Rhythm of the Day/Buddy's Habits; Hurricane; Boneyard Shuffle; Alexander's Ragtime Band; Mean Dog Blues; Alabama Stomp; Riverboat Shuffle; Cornfed; Eccentric; Feelin' No Pain; Corrina Corrine; Original Dixieland One-Step; Honolulu Blues; and seven others. Living Era AJA/CDAJA-5025 (LP/CD).

Several of Nichols's phrase shapes—for instance, in "Boneyard Shuffle" and "Feelin' No Pain"—sound curiously like Miles Davis. One should also note, in a few selections, the replacement of Dorsey with **Charles "Pee Wee" Russell** (1906–1969), a maverick clarinetist whose sometimes infirm, "fugitive" tone annoyed some and thrilled others. In addition to the above titles, which amply demonstrate Nichols's experimentation, the unusual configurations in "That's No Bargain" (MCA 1518E) show a treatment of rhythm that seems to have no set pulse. Indeed, for half the record it is difficult to tell the off-beats from the principal ones. Such experimentation preceded Teddy Hill, John Kirby, and Thelonious Monk by at least a decade.

While some musicians were dabbling in exotic, European-based harmonies and exploring new, virtuosic uses of the cornet, trombone, and violin in jazz, others were defining the jazz use of the saxophone. Never considered a vehicle for jazz solos in New Orleans (except for the soprano sax, which sometimes substitued for the clarinet), the various members of the sax family were left to the province of commercial dance bands and vaudeville players, where slap-tonguing was considered high art. By the late 1920s, two extraordinary musicians were breaking free of the non-jazz stigma attached to their instruments: **Johnny Hodges** (1902–1970) on the alto and **Coleman Hawkins** (1904–1969) on the tenor.

Hodges, of course, came to fame in the Duke Ellington orchestra (to be discussed later), but of all Duke's great soloists of the period none had as big an influence on the emerging jazz generation as "Rabbit." In his early discs there is some trace of the slap-tongue technique, but as early as 1929 one can hear it disappearing. Benny Carter, one of the musicians Hodges influenced most, was even smoother at that time, yet it is apparent that Hodges "wrote the book," as they say, on his instrument. His use of smoothly integrated triplets in his improvising, combined with a tone always perfectly centered and in tune (regardless of how cold the hall was—something other sax players never quite got over), made him the hallmark altoist until the advent of Charlie Parker.

In fact, Hodges even influenced Hawkins, who had an even more difficult time molding his instrument for jazz usage. It may seem hard for some of us today to believe, but in the 1920s the tenor was never considered a melody instrument. Hawkins made it so, but the birth pains of his search for a style are evident on his early recordings. In the 1924–1925 Henderson band, his tone was already full but his phrasing was jerky in a jazz sense, replete with vaudevillian effects such as rolling triplets. By 1928–1929, largely due to the example of Hodges, Hawkins's style was becoming smoother, more flowing, and cohesive. He would not enter his great period until the early 1930s, but he was well on his way to revolutionizing his instrument.

There was also an obscure Chicago pianist, **Clarence "Pine Top" Smith** (1904–1929), who introduced the next great piano style of the 1920s after Johnson and Hines. Boogie-woogie, based on the blues and emphasizing a continuously thumping bass, emigrated from the South (primarily Texas) but gained its popularity through Smith. He made just a handful of records, all of which fill the second side of *Piano in Style*, MCA/MCAC-1332, LP/Cs (OP): "I'm Sober Now," "Nobody Knows You," and two takes each of "Pinetop's Boogie-Woogie," "Pinetop's Blues," and "Jump Steady Blues." His "vocals"—primarily speaking the lyrics over his piano playing—tend to be hokey, but the playing, by contrast, is curiously fluid, fluent, and highly sophisticated. One will not find the banging and thumping of Pete Johnson or Albert Ammons here, but a wonderfully relaxed and imaginative musical treatment. The bass fairly rebounds off the walls with gaiety, passing through changes that would never have occurred to most boogie players, and the rhythm is more jazzy than mechanical.

As we prepare to leave the period from 1924 to 1931, there is one more giant to discuss, to whom we'll return several times. **Edward "Duke" Ellington** (1899–1974) represented a summation of jazz in all periods from here on, the way

Morton did for New Orleans. Ellington's first band was formed in 1924, with banjoist Elmer Snowden, but it was only after Ellington took full possession of it in late 1925 that it began to develop into a unique unit. The first great recordings were made in 1927–1928, as can be sampled below:

> *Early Ellington*/Black and Tan Fantasy; East St. Louis Too-dle-Oo; Creole Love Call; Black Beauty; Cotton Club Stomp; The Mooche; Flaming Youth; Ring Dem Bells; Old Man Blues; Mood Indigo; Rockin' in Rhythm; Creole Rhapsody; and Echoes of the Jungle—from the 1927–1931 period, plus others. RCA Bluebird 6852-1/2/4-RB (LP/CD/Cs).

> *The Ellington Era, Vol. 1*/Black and Tan Fantasy; East St. Louis Toodle-Oo; Hop Head; Jubilee Stomp; The Mooche; Lazy Duke; Hot and Bothered; Blues With a Feeling; Old Man Blues; Mood Indigo; Rockin' in Rhythm; and It Don't Mean a Thing—from this era— plus thirty-six others. Columbia C3L-27 (LP, OP).

As the discs show, this was a first-rate jazz orchestra by any standard. Unlike Henderson's, the Ellington sound was built not on offset sections but on the interwoven playing of extraordinary individuals. Even within this four-year span, we can hear trumpeters Bubber Miley, Jabbo Smith, and Cootie Williams, trombonists Joe "Tricky Sam" Nanton and Juan Tizol, saxists Hodges and Harry Carney, clarinetist Barney Bigard, bassist Wellman Braud, and drummer Sonny Greer. This curious concoction of New Orleans players (Bigard, Smith, and Braud), hot blues men (Miley and Nanton), and "new"-style musicians (Hodges and Williams) made for a unique melting pot. That Ellington was able to pull these diverse elements together, let alone produce great music, testifies to his genius.

A few numbers were, obviously, remade for different labels. There is not much difference between the two versions of "Mood Indigo" or "Black and Tan Fantasy," but the others are quite different. The Columbia version of "East St. Louis," for instance, is faster, with the swing more aggressive and a tuba replacing the bowed string bass, and the OKeh version of "The Mooche" contains a scat vocal by Baby Cox.

Far and away the most amazing record, however, is the Victor version of "Creole Love Call." This simple but hypnotic blues, played mostly by a clarinet trio, contains an interwoven scat vocal by Adelaide Hall. What makes it unusual is that the vocal line isn't something extraneous, but an important and integral part of the composition. Without it, the piece just doesn't sound right, as demonstrated by Ellington's later (and largely unsuccessful) remakes. The sound of the clarinets, incidentally, was one of his few stylistic hallmarks. Ellington retained them in his orchestra up to the very end, long after the instrument had lost its supremacy as a solo jazz voice to the saxophone.

There were very few times when social or economic conditions imposed themselves on the creation of new styles or the forward movement of jazz, but the first years of the Great Depression was one of them. Independent sessions by small groups became rare—for some years, the handful of major record companies played it safe, with large orchestras playing bland pop music, and the small labels died out or were swallowed up by bigger ones. Still, a few major talents managed to surface during those years, make an impact, and help set the stage for jazz's reemergence in 1936.

3.
Depression

The prosperity of the 1920s—however short-lived—had encouraged the growth of jazz. Though the names of Beiderbecke, Morton, Henderson, and Ellington were not as well known to the general public as Paul Whiteman, George Olsen, Roger Wolfe Kahn, or the Coon-Sanders Nighthawks, even the last two named produced music that was jazz-influenced. Whiteman even hired Beiderbecke, Trumbauer, Venuti, Lang, Berton, Nichols, and the Dorsey brothers. As the Depression deepened, however, most Americans began to reject the happy sounds of jazz-influenced pop, preferring more soothing, syrupy, genteel music.

Unfortunately, 1930 saw the last of Beiderbecke, Bubber Miley, and the Red Hot Peppers in the recording studios, and the last Nichols jazz session for many years. Ellington took his superb band to England in 1933. In 1934, faced with lack of work, Fletcher Henderson's group simply disbanded. Until his death in 1933, Eddie Lang left the insecurity of pickup sessions to work with Bing Crosby in Hollywood, while Goodman, Venuti, and the Dorseys fled to the security of studio work and Teagarden joined Whiteman. Nichols turned to Broadway shows, organizing an all-star jazz band for Gershwin's *Girl Crazy* that included most of the above names, plus Glenn Miller and Gene Krupa.

Curiously, at about the same time that most Americans were coming to prefer the soothing syrup of commercial ballads, a group of musicians were changing forever the role of the big band in jazz. This was the Casa Loma Orchestra, fronted by a handsome sax player who had changed his name from Glen Knoblaugh to **Glen Gray** (1900–1963); yet the majority of their ear-catching arrangements were written by **Eugene Gifford**, a little-known banjoist and guitarist who had worked during the late 1920s with a group called the Orange Blossoms.

Gifford took the jerky Charleston beat of the 1920s, smoothed it out into something far more syncopated and jazzy, and then wrote dazzling virtuoso passages for the trumpets and saxes. These, in turn, were executed with a precision and bite hitherto unknown in jazz. Sometimes the staccato passages verged on choppiness, but in all Gifford lay the groundwork for a new band style. He alternated the up-tempo numbers with slow, dreamy "mood" pieces such as "Smoke Rings" and "Under a Blanket of Blue," which were more pop-oriented but featured some excellent solos to offset the lugubrious crooning of the band's singer, Kenny Sargent. The best of their 1930–1934 output may be found in the following album:

> *Best of the Big Bands: Glen Gray*/Smoke Rings; Black Jazz; Tired of It All; Maniac's Ball; Clarinet Marmalade; For You; Dixie Lee; Casa Loma Stomp; Under a Blanket of Blue; I Got Rhythm; New Orleans; Here Come the British; My Man; Ol' Man River; Shadows of Love; and Limehouse Blues. CBS CK/CT-45345 (CD/Cs).

Especially notable among the soloists were clarinet/alto saxist Clarence Hutchenrider, trombonist/sometimes vocalist Pee Wee Hunt, and trumpeter Sonny Dunham. One oddity that seems to have been pioneered by Casa Loma, and that has received little or no comment, is that the rhythm section played together so that the guitar, piano, bass, and drums functioned as a unit. Prior to their arrival, even in the Fletcher

Henderson band, the rhythm section was often broken up: bass and drums, or piano and guitar, or piano and drums. This was an influence from New Orleans jazz in general, and Jelly Roll Morton in particular, which was done to add variety to the sound-color. The white Chicagoans were the first to attempt this rhythmic integration in small-band jazz; Casa Loma was the first to do so in big-band jazz, giving the sections and soloists a solid cushion over which to work. Casa Loma proved especially popular with the college kids—that is, whatever college kids were left after the Wall Street crash. By the time that audience faded, however, the band was a firm favorite on records and radio. They may well be said to have paved the way for the swing era that followed.

One band that Casa Loma had a beneficial effect on was the organization led by singer **Cab Calloway** (1907–), which followed Duke Ellington into the Cotton Club. Cab Calloway was different from any other singer who had preceded him: He had a silver trumpet of a voice, operatic range and projection, superb diction, and an ability to scat second only to Armstrong. At times the showman in Calloway superseded the jazz musician, with the result that about half of what he sang was a sort of jivey pop music; but the other half was pure jazz, and excellent jazz at that.

The band itself, as already noted, was strongly influenced by Casa Loma as well as Fletcher Henderson. It had its share of star players, from trumpeters Lammar Wright and Doc Cheatham to (in the early 1940s) Dizzy Gillespie. Their sense of style was never a strong point—one suspects that Cab preferred that the band's most distinctive sound was his own voice—yet he often deferred to his instrumentalists as few other singers have ever done. As a result, they maintained a highly swinging profile in all their years together, which the following album amply shows:

   Best of the Big Bands: Cab Calloway/Minnie the Moocher; Beale Street Mama; Angeline; Minnie the Moocher's Wed-

ding Day; Dinah; You Gotta Ho-Di-Ho; Reefer Man; Man-
hattan Jam; Eadie Was a Lady; Take the "A" Train; F.D.R.
Jones; Bye Bye Blues; Wake Up and Live; Pickin' the
Cabbage; The Jumpin' Jive; and I Gotta Go Places and
Do Things. CBS CK/CT-45336 (CD/Cs).

In the above album, the last seven selections date from the
late 1930s or early 1940s and should be set aside until our
discussion of the swing era; even though this version of "Minnie the Moocher" dates from 1942, it is a timeless arrangement that never changed from the time Cab first introduced
it in 1930.

Like Glen Gray, the Calloway band fared well in the early
Depression years, in his case primarily because the leader was
such a superb showman. One Casa Loma–influenced band
that was a major casualty of the era, however, was the magnificent group led by pianist **Bennie Moten** (1894–1935), out
of Kansas City. The band included such major jazz names as
Count Basie, Oran "Hot Lips" Page, Ben Webster, Jimmy
Rushing, and Walter Page, yet seldom got farther east than
Chicago. One of the few times they did was in 1931, when
they played the Pearl Theater in Philadelphia—following
Fletcher Henderson! The gig was such a success that they
tried it again the following year, but this time, whether due
to miscalculation or someone's outright dishonesty, the band
never got paid. In desperation, Moten hastily arranged a
recording session with RCA Victor to make enough money
to get his bandsmen back home. The records they made are
classics, yet they barely sold at the time. The following album
contains their best jazz sides:

Bennie Moten's Kansas City Orchestra/The Jones Law Blues;
Small Black; Every Day Blues; Rit-Dit-Ray; New Vine
Street Blues; Oh! Eddie; Sweetheart of Yesterday; Won't
You Be My Baby; That Too, Do Blues; The Count; Liza
Lee; When I'm Alone; New Moten Stomp; Somebody
Stole My Gal; Now That I Need You; Toby; Moten Swing;
The Blue Room; New Orleans; Milenberg Joys; Lafayette;

and Prince of Wales. RCA Bluebird 9768-1/2/4-RB (LP/CD/Cs).

Almost every track on this remarkable album is a good one. Their last records, the 1932 sides ("Toby" through "Prince of Wales"), are particularly outstanding. And despite the widespread indifference toward jazz in this era, some major talents either came up or made new starts in the early-to-mid-1930s. We shall examine some of the best to get an overview of development in the midst of struggle.

During his stint as arranger for McKinney's Cotton Pickers (1928–1931), Don Redman made a group of recordings under the *nom de disque* of the Chocolate Dandies, utilizing arrangements by himself and trumpeter John Nesbitt. Dandies recordings continued to emerge during the Depression, and one of the most remarkable talents to emerge in this later group was that of **Benny Carter** (1907–), a multitalented figure whose work as trumpeter, alto saxist, clarinetist, and arranger left many scratching their heads as to how to categorize him. There was no way to do so, however, except to say that Carter's playing was the first (after Beiderbecke's) to bear no trace at all of the somewhat jerky 1920s rhythm. He always possessed an unfettered fluidity in his improvisations that, like Beiderbecke's, remains timeless in or out of the context of the surrounding musicians.

Fortunately, however, the Dandies had some wonderful mixed talent, including Hendersonians Hawkins, Harrison, and Rex Stewart; New Yorkers Fats Waller, Teddy Wilson, and Chu Berry; New Orleans–styled J. C. Higginbotham and Sid Catlett; and white Chicagoans Max Kaminsky and Floyd O'Brien. All can be heard on the following album, in a conglomeration of music that ranges from loosely arranged jam sessions to big-band swing of a fairly high order that bears the Carter touch:

The Chocolate Dandies, 1928–33/Cherry; Paducah; Stardust; Birmingham Breakdown; Four or Five Times;

That's How I Feel Today; Six or Seven Times; Goodbye
Blues; Cloudy Skies; Got Another Sweetie Now; Bugle Call
Rag; Dee Blues; Blue Interlude; I Never Knew; Once
Upon a Time; and Krazy Kapers. DRG/Disques Swing
CDSW-8448 (CD).

Working side by side with Carter and Nesbitt as arranger
for the Dandies was Don Redman, who by the time of the
later sides had left McKinney's Cotton Pickers and was leading his own big band. Redman, however, was unaffected by
the revolutions of Casa Loma: He preferred to pursue a
warm, rich-sounding ensemble highlighted by his own arrangements, those of Fletcher Henderson's brother Horace,
and an especially superb trombone section of Claude Jones,
Fred Robinson, and Benny Morton. In the album *Don Redman
and his Orchestra, 1931–1933* (Classics 543), one can hear such
outstanding cuts as "Shakin' the African" and "I Heard," in
which Redman's quaint habit of "speaking" lyrics is alternated
with some hot ensemble and solo playing; "Trouble, Why
Pick On Me," where a rather dated vocal is followed by some
exciting double-time trumpet from Henry "Red" Allen; and
his classic "Chant of the Weed," in which bitonal harmonies
are fused with a swinging beat to produce one of the early
classics of orchestrated jazz.

At the very time that Carter and Redman were progressing
stylistically, Louis Armstrong was stuck in one of his few ruts.
Whether the result of an inspirational backlash from the
brilliance of the 1925–1929 period, or a conscious desire to
be a pop entertainer rather than a pure jazz artist, there is
no question that the 1930–1934 period was one of artistic
stagnation for Armstrong. He had Luis Russell form a band
for him as a backdrop for his singing and playing, which he
alternated with other orchestras. That band style, by Louis'
own insistence, bore an unhappy resemblance to Guy Lom-
bardo's Royal Canadians, thus robbing his music of much
virility. As a soloist, Armstrong tended to repeat patterns he
had created in the previous decade, and became somewhat
wayward and flamboyant at the expense of intelligent crea-

tion. After a while, the only real interest in Armstrong was how many high C's he could cram into a chorus, a venture which hurt his lip. With a few exceptions (among them "Ding Dong Daddy from Dumas," "You Rascal You," "Dinah," "Little Joe," and "Between the Devil and the Deep Blue Sea"), his records from this period are to be avoided, though ironically they made him famous.

One of the last New Orleans jazz giants returned to the United States in 1930, from his travels in France and Russia, as a member of Noble Sissle's Orchestra. This was **Sidney Bechet** (1897–1959), absolute master of the soprano saxophone (and clarinet), jazz's most rhapsodic soloist. He'd made a few acoustic discs with Armstrong in 1924 (see *Jazz Vol. 3*), but these scarcely did Bechet justice. In 1932 he formed a group with trumpeter Tommy Ladnier, the New Orleans Feetwarmers, which turned out a short but superb series of discs that put Bechet on the musical map.

Considering the fire and improvisatory spirit of these recordings, they bear an amazing resemblance in style, execution, and interplay to the Red Hot Peppers. But as Morton himself said, Bechet was one of the "greatest dispensers of jazz" around. Three of these discs (the first three listed) are in the following CD:

> *The Legendary Sidney Bechet*/Maple Leaf Rag; I've Found a New Baby; Weary Blues; Really the Blues; High Society; Indian Summer; Shake It and Break It; Sidney's Blues; Wild Man Blues; Save It, Pretty Mama; Stompy Jones; Muskrat Ramble; The Sheik of Araby; Baby, Won't You Please Come Home; I'm Comin', Virginia; The Mooche; When It's Sleepy Time Down South; Strange Fruit; Blues in the Air; 12th Street Rag; Mood Indigo; and What Is This Thing Called Love. RCA Bluebird 6590-1/2/4-RB (LP/CD/Cs).

In addition to tunes by the New Orleans Feetwarmers, this album is valuable for a number of fairly modern, non-New Orleans settings. Unlike many players from the Crescent City, Bechet could adapt to advanced swing and early bop settings.

Indeed, he wouldn't have been out of place in Ellington's band at its most progressive, as his modernistic renditions of "Blues in the Air" and "The Mooche" testify. Bechet played the saxophone in a way unlike any other practitioner on earth. He would attack notes with the boldness and clarity of a trumpet, digging and growing when called for while never sacrificing musicality for the sake of effect. He also used an unusually strong vibrato, which he could pick apart and ride on with the expertise of a high-wire walker. In addition to all this, his harmonic daring was truly virtuosic; one gets the feeling that Bechet could improvise on "Yankee Doodle" and make great jazz out of it.

In short, Bechet's playing, though inherently old-fashioned because of the insistent vibrato, was amazingly flexible in its stylistic use. When he returned to a New Orleans format in the late 1940s it wasn't, as with Kid Ory, just because that was all he could play, but simply a matter of choice by a master who had already proven he could do it all. In 1957, toward the end of his life, he made an album with progressive French pianist Martial Solal which indicates that had he lived, he might even have been able to play with Miles Davis and John Coltrane. Sidney Bechet remains the greatest all-round lead horn in the history of jazz.

Less adaptable, but just as spectacular within limits, was the playing of trumpeter **Roland "Bunny" Berigan** (1908–1942), who to this day remains the only white player to follow in Armstrong's musical footsteps and yet produce something truly original. His playing may be heard on any number of studio sessions of the early 1930s— "I'm Comin', Virginia" is on *Jazz Vol. 11*—as well as on several big-band recordings by Benny Goodman and Tommy Dorsey. An excellent cross section of his lyrical trumpet style, which explored the lower register better than anyone with the exception of Ruby Braff, may be heard in the following:

Portrait of Bunny Berigan/Me Minus You; She Reminds Me of You; Troubled; Plantation Moods; In a Little Spanish

Town; Solo Hop; Nothin' But the Blues; Squareface; King
Porter Stomp; The Buzzard; Tillie's Downtown Now; You
Took Advantage of Me; Chicken and Waffles; I'm Comin',
Virginia; Blues; Swing, Mister Charlie; Blue Lou; Marie;
Black Bottom; The Prisoner's Song; and I Can't Get
Started. ASV/Living Era AJA/CDAJA-5060 (LP/CD).

In the above compilation, Berigan is heard in context with
the studio bands of Glenn Miller and Bud Freeman; on the
famous Goodman recording of "King Porter Stomp"; on the
equally famous Tommy Dorsey recording of "Marie"; and
on Berigan's greatest masterpiece, the recording of "I Can't
Get Started" with his own band. In addition to these, he can
be heard in context with Red Norvo, Mildred Bailey, Billie
Holiday, and the following vocal group, which was the first
of its kind in jazz history.

The Boswell Sisters—Connee, Vet, and Martha—had
made a name for themselves in New Orleans, then on radio
in California, before being broadcast nationally on CBS.
Though some of their records were in a soothing pop style,
there remains enough exciting material to earn them a berth
in jazz history. On record, they were often teamed with the
Dorsey brothers, who hired Berigan, Manny Klein, Artie
Bernstein, Venuti, Lang, and several other fine jazzmen to
produce a sort of slick New Orleans style behind them as
they sang. Today that band style sounds a little hokey and
contrived, but not so the solo work of Jimmy and Tommy
Dorsey, Berigan, Klein, Venuti, et al., nor the vocal stylings
of the sisters.

What made the Boswells unique was that they were the
first group to use "crossover" harmony—which is to say, they
didn't always harmonize in a set position of bottom-to-top
voice. Though Connee was usually in the middle, with Vet
on top and Martha beneath, they often changed vocal positions within a phrase or even a bar. They also had a superb
sense of rhythm, which today makes their drummers and
pianists sound inadequate by comparison. Indeed, only the

guitarists—Lang and McDonough—sound as modern in concept (of the rhythm) as they do. The following album covers much of their best work:

> *Everybody Loves My Baby*/Heebie Jeebies; River, Stay 'Way from My Door; Wha'd Ja Do to Me?; When I Take My Sugar to Tea; Roll On, Mississippi, Roll On; Shout, Sister, Shout; It's the Girl; Lawd, You Made the Night Too Long (w/ Bing Crosby); Shuffle Off to Buffalo; Everybody Loves My Baby; Hand Me Down My Walking Cane; There'll Be Some Changes Made; Mood Indigo; Sentimental Gentleman from Georgia; Old Yazoo; The Devil and the Deep Blue Sea; 'Way Back Home; and 42nd Street. Pro Arte CDD-550 (CD).

Three of the above items—"River Stay 'Way," "Lawd, You Made the Night," and "Way Back Home"—are essentially pop performances of then-standard material, with very little variating in the jazz sense (though Don Redman's Orchestra is also on "Lawd"). But the others, in varying degrees, show the Boswells' absolute mastery of jazz form.

The average Boswell record had at least three abrupt (and perfectly executed) tempo changes, key or mode changes, and a variance on rhythm with which they'd swing to the breaking point. Connee's rich contralto would alternate solos with the trio, and though hers was obviously the finest voice, they'd blend so well that one couldn't always pick hers out. Connee's singing, incidentally, represents the first female scatting in jazz history. Mildred Bailey, often considered the first female jazz singer, earned that plaudit largely through her impeccable sense of rhythm and certain inflections of phrasing, but Connee could scat like an alto sax player.

As time went on, the Boswells modernized their style somewhat, singing a few lines in unison rather than harmonizing, but either way, they exerted a powerful influence, not only on the later Lambert, Hendricks, and Ross—who also used crossover harmony in the bop idiom—but also on the early Pointer Sisters.

Another outstanding soloist of the era, and one who (like

Bunny Berigan) was too restless to stay with any one band for too long, was tenor saxist **Bud Freeman** (1906–1991). A refugee from the old Austin High Gang, Freeman was not (like Coleman Hawkins) a superb saxophonist who played jazz; he was a jazzman who happened to play the tenor sax. He approached his instrument with no sense of its history or contemporary usage—he merely put it to his lips and blew. As a result, his tone was full-bodied but somewhat rough, though its roughness in the beginning was the result of improper blowing technique. As he refined his playing in the 1930s, however, he was able to enlarge the scope of his improvisations. By 1933 he was playing such difficult and convoluted pieces of his own devising as "The Eel," "The Buzzard," and "The Sail Fish," which used the old vaudeville triplet technique in an entirely valid, jazzy way. For a couple of years he played with the white society band of Britisher Ray Noble, then spent stints in the bands of Tommy Dorsey and Benny Goodman. Freeman was happier with Dorsey, who featured him in his small band-within-a-band, the Clambake Seven, but longed for his own outfit. Thus, near the end of 1938, he formed the Summa Cum Laude Orchestra, a small group that featured fellow Chicagoans Max Kaminsky (trumpet) and **Pee Wee Russell** (1906–1969), one of the most individualistic clarinetists who ever lived.

Freeman's early style can be heard in "Nobody's Sweetheart" on *Chicago* (BBC REB/CD/ZCF-589, LP/CD/Cs) and in "Barnacle Bill the Sailor" on *Bix Beiderbecke* (see Chapter 2). In addition, he plays both clarinet and tenor sax on the Bunny Berigan CD (Living Era CDAJA-5060). Four tracks by the Summa Cum Laude Orchestra, including "The Eel" and "I've Found a New Baby," are on *At the Jazz Band Ball* (RCA Bluebird 6752-2-RB, CD). Russell's quirky yet fascinating clarinet style is also evident in the last-mentioned tunes.

The 1930s also saw the reemergence, in a big way, of a Harlem stride pianist who had studied with James P. Johnson but created his own style, a startling cross between tasteful musician and crowd-pleasing showman. This was **Thomas**

"Fats" Waller (1904–1943) who, like Morton, Henderson, and his mentor Johnson, lapsed into obscurity at the beginning of the Depression, only to emerge phoenixlike in 1934 with the first of a long line of recordings with His Rhythm. Here was something new: bad Tin Pan Alley songs, often of a sentimental nature, swung to the limit with mocking vocals by Fats, thus made to stand up to the most stringent jazz standards. And then, of course, there were his original compositions, songs such as "Handful of Keys," "Squeeze Me," "Ain't Misbehavin'," and "Honeysuckle Rose," which helped make him a big popular favorite.

There are many fine examples of his work available, both on American labels and French reissues, but the following album will serve as well as any to introduce his unique genius to the uninitiated:

> *The Definitive Fats Waller, Vol. 1*/Baby Brown; Viper's Drag; How Can You Face Me?; Down Home Blues; Dinah (two vers.); Handful of Keys (two vers.); Solitude; The Moon Is Low (two tks.); The Sheik of Araby; E Flat Blues; Honeysuckle Rose (two tks.); Ain't Misbehavin'; Sweet Sue; Nagasaki; I'm Crazy 'Bout My Baby; The Spider and the Fly; Lonesome Me; After You've Gone (two tks.); Poor Butterfly; St. Louis Blues; Hallclujah; and Tea for Two. Stash ST-CD-528 (CD).

Almost any selection here will show what Waller could do to a pop song, but the effervescent "Sheik of Araby" and the surreal "Spider and the Fly" are particularly noteworthy. So is Waller's pianism: no crude barrelhouse, but a superb locked-hands stride that makes musical sense even at the most nonsensical moment, and even has elements of tenderness and melancholy. Fans of the 1980s Broadway revue *Ain't Misbehavin'* will also recognize songs used in the show, such as "Viper's Drag," "Handful of Keys," "Honeysuckle Rose," and the title tune.

The early 1930s also saw an increased sophistication in big-band playing, as witness the influence of Casa Loma. The somewhat jerky Charleston/ragtime beat was disappearing, and so, too, were the banjo and the tuba, to be replaced by guitar and string bass. Henderson was the first to accomplish this, in 1930, when bassist John Kirby came into the band to join guitarist Clarence Holiday. But, as usual, it was Ellington who seized on the new sophistication and utilized it to maximum advantage. In some of the earliest tracks, Fred Guy plays his guitar with hard, banjo-like strokes, but by late 1933 and early 1934, his playing had become much smoother.

Some superb examples from this era are included in the two albums recommended in Chapter 2. On *Early Ellington* (RCA) is the first, superior version of "Solitude," with a majestic Cootie Williams solo; the equally beautiful "Delta Serenade"; and "Daybreak Express," with its wild, highly imaginative scoring. *The Ellington Era* (Columbia) contains a number of groundbreaking recordings: "It Don't Mean a Thing (If It Ain't Got That Swing)," "Lazy Rhapsody," "Blue Harlem," "Sheik of Araby," "Lightnin'," "Blue Ramble," "Ducky Wucky," "Drop Me Off in Harlem," "Bundle O' Blues," "Slippery Horn," "Harlem Speaks," and "Merry-Go-Round." Again, all are fine examples of his work, but particular interest centers on "It Don't Mean a Thing," with its ooh-wah brass, aggressive Ivie Anderson vocal, and fine alto chorus by Johnny Hodges; "Lazy Rhapsody," with a warm scat vocal by Cootie Williams; "Sheik of Araby," which includes Lawrence Brown's fine trombone; "Harlem Speaks," which features unusual chording and a whirling performance; and "Merry-Go-Round," which introduces Rex Stewart as a defector from the defunct Henderson band.

The last-named performance reminds us that the big-band era was but a beat or two away. Indeed, the joy and enthusiasm of the record make it hard to realize that it wasn't yet (pardon the pun) in full swing.

Before we cross that giant hurdle between 1935 and 1936, however, we must first pay tribute to two more giants of the music. First we go to Europe, where we discover the only French jazzman to influence Americans. This was the Gypsy guitarist **Django Reinhardt** (1910–1953), who, along with violinist **Stephane Grappelli** (1908–), founded the legendary Quintet of the Hot Club of France. Their feeling was, if the records Venuti and Lang made by themselves were good, more string instruments would be better. So they fronted a drummerless group where Reinhardt's guitar and Grappelli's violin were backed by two more guitars and a string bass. Their sound was light and airy, with plenty of solo room for the two stars, and Reinhardt's playing quite literally turned heads around in astonishment.

Here for the first time was a guitarist whose single-note playing wasn't limited to occasional breaks, but given full rein in choruses in which his steely, aggressive attack and dazzling technique made him fully the equal of any pianist or horn player. He could play hard downstrokes on his chords, which gave him something of the old banjo quality, but more often than not Reinhardt's percussive rhythm was closer to the concept of a drummer. He also darted through dazzling runs utilizing upper harmonics and overtones in a way that predated the bop revolution of the 1940s. Though no less a personage than Ellington rated him one of the four greatest soloists in jazz history (Armstrong and Bechet were two others—we'll meet the fourth in a moment), Reinhardt's lone U.S. tour, with Ellington's band in 1946, was a disaster. Reinhardt, frightened and ill-prepared, played the poorest guitar of his career. The following two albums give a much better impression of what had shell-shocked the jazz fraternity in 1934 and 1935:

Django '35–'39/Limehouse Blues; I Got Rhythm; St. Louis Blues; I've Found a New Baby; It Was So Beautiful; China Boy; It Don't Mean a Thing; Moonglow; Billets Doux; Swing From Paris; Three Little Words; Appel Direct; Them There Eyes; and Swing '39. GNP Crescendo GNP-9019 (LP).

The Legendary Django Reinhardt/Dark Eyes; Minor Swing; How High the Moon; Place de Broukère; St. Louis Blues;

Tiger Rag; Dinah; Symphonie; Belleville; Them There
Eyes; Improvisation; Swing Dynamique. GNP Crescendo
GNP-9039 (LP).

On the first LP, one will note how the somewhat conservative approach of the earlier cuts give way by 1939 to full-
throttle swinging, as well as Reinhardt's incredible guitar
technique. On "Appel Direct," for example, he plays a solo
that many guitarists consider impossible. The second album
has some rare late recordings of Reinhardt from his electric-
guitar, bop-style days ("Place de Broukère," "Swing Dynamique," and "Symphonie") that stand up to the best work of
such American guitarists as Charlie Christian and Barney
Kessel. On both discs are samples of Reinhardt's interesting
compositional style, the most intriguing works being "Appel
Direct," "Swing From Paris," and "Belleville."

The last jazz giant to emerge from this era is the fourth
man Duke Ellington called one of the "preeminent soloists"
of our time; many critics consider him the greatest jazz musician of our century, regardless of instrument. This was **Art
Tatum** (1910–1956), a pianist of such rare accomplishment
and influence that the remainder of this chapter is devoted
to him.

Originally trained as a concert pianist, Tatum found little
latitude in 1928 for poor blacks in the classical field. Spurned
by the Juilliard and Manhattan schools of music when he
applied for scholarships, Tatum played in and around his
native Toledo, in clubs and on the radio. Word soon leaked
out about a young man who could outplay any pianist alive,
but he didn't achieve popularity until 1932, when he came
to New York as accompanist for singer Adelaide Hall. Here,
in the traditional spirit of "cutting contests," Tatum patiently
waited until James P. Johnson, Willie the Lion, and Fats
Waller did their best at the keyboard, then sat down and
quietly blew them away.

What made Tatum unique was not his technique—though
it was the finest in jazz (Godowsky and Horowitz both ad-

mired it), capable of producing sixty-fourth-note flurries in perfect time through some of the most difficult changes on the keyboard—but his ability to improvise the melody, harmony, and rhythm *simultaneously*. Earl Hines, whose free-style was one of Art's major influences, helped pave the way in his unusual broken-rhythm solo work, but Tatum took this much farther. In a Tatum solo, a substitute chord would be accompanied by a right-hand improvisation on the principal tune, while his fractioning of rhythm could take place within a bar, a half bar, or one beat. Listening critically to more than twenty minutes of Tatum at a stretch has one ill effect, however: It is so dense that it can give some listeners a headache!

In the beginning, Tatum was content to let the dazzle of his technical mastery overwhelm the listener, but by the late 1930s his style had evolved considerably. Nevertheless, he was inhibited by Jack Kapp, founder of Decca Records (to whom he was under contract), who did not like dense improvisations and so restricted Tatum's playing time to mere melodic embellishments. Not until the late 1940s did Columbia and Capitol capture Tatum's style the way he wanted it. In the early 1950s, Norman Granz signed Tatum to an exclusive contract with his Verve label, and set aside whole weeks for the master to record his repertoire. Tatum filled thirteen LPs with his solo piano, but Granz still wasn't satisfied. He then teamed Tatum with such first-class instrumentalist as Benny Carter, Harry Edison, Lionel Hampton, Barney Kessel, Buddy de Franco, Buddy Rich, and Louis Bellson to fill eight more albums. *The Tatum Solo Masterpieces*, now in a boxed set on Pablo, is recommended to those who wish to pursue his playing in full, but the three LPs listed below give an excellent cross section; and the first four titles on the Columbia album are his first records, from 1933:

Piano Starts Here/Tea for Two; St. Louis Blues; Sophisticated Lady; Tiger Rag; How High the Moon; Someone to Watch Over Me; Humoresque; Yesterdays; I Know

That You Know; Willow, Weep for Me; Tatum Pole Boogie; Kerry Dance; and The Man I Love. Columbia CS/PCT-9655E (LP/Cs).

The Complete Capitol Recordings, Vol. 1/Willow, Weep for Me; I Cover the Waterfront; Aunt Hagar's Blues; Nice Work If You Can Get It; Someone to Watch Over Me; Dardanella; Time on My Hands; Sweet Lorraine; Somebody Loves Me; Don't Blame Me; September Song; Melody in F; Tea for Two; and Out of Nowhere. Capitol CDP-92866 (CD).

Tatum-Carter-Bellson/Blues in C; Undecided; Under a Blanket of Blue; Blues in B Flat; A Foggy Day; Street of Dreams; 'Swonderful; Makin' Whoopee; Old-Fashioned Love; I'm Left With the Blues in My Heart; My Blue Heaven; Hands Across the Table; You're Mine You; and Idaho. Pablo 2310/52310-732/733, 2405-424-2 (two LPs/Cs, one CD).

There is some duplication of material in the first two LPs, which shows how little his approach to a song changed once he'd found the way: For instance, note that the different versions of "Someone to Watch Over Me" and "Willow, Weep for Me" are practically identical in the changes and direction selected. Of course, this only fuels the fires of those who refuse to accept Tatum as a true jazz musician, but as we've seen, this particular criticism doesn't hold water. It took a mastermind to find such directions in the first place and, as the ensemble recordings prove, that mind never really stopped working, even when as many as five other musicians are providing distractions. Tatum's reliance on glissandi can be predictable, but there was a reason for them. Because he was three-quarters blind, it helped him negotiate from one end of the keyboard to the other with better speed and accuracy than might otherwise have been possible for him.

Perhaps the three finest examples of his improvisatory skills are "Yesterdays," "Aunt Hagar's Blues," and "Idaho." In the first, he transforms the melody into a richly romantic classical intro, à la Franz Liszt, then introduces a flowing boogie bass for the bridge when the speed increases, and finally lands in a nice, swinging tempo before retreating to a classical ending. In "Aunt Hagar's Blues" he subtly and skillfully overlays the popular song "Black Coffee" onto W. C. Handy's original melody, making it an integral part of the overall recomposition. The effect is magical, producing a deceptively simple and moody performance.

If the first two recordings exemplify astonishing powers of technique, harmonic complexity, and musical sublimination, "Idaho" reveals just how powerful his creative powers really were. Here Benny Carter's alto sax solo is followed by a positive flurry of notes from the pianist that builds and builds until the listener is convinced that Carter will never be able to reenter without damaging the flow. Surprisingly, what ensues is a sort of simultaneous chase-chorus, with both soloists somehow finding "holes" in the other's playing to complement and compete with at the same time. Moments like this give the lie to jazz's so-called simplicity and reveal it for the extraordinarily complex music it really is.

Toward the middle of 1935 jazz's greatest clarinetist, Benny Goodman, suddenly created a furor in California with his big swing band. By stubbornly keeping the group alive a few weeks longer than he'd planned, he managed to usher in a new jazz era single-handedly. Some have damned him for it, others have praised him, but none deny that he made jazz the foremost form of popular music for the first and last time in this century.

4.
Swing, Brother, Swing!

If the 1920s was a decade in which a great deal of hokiness and popular styles were blended with jazz, the "swing era" (1935–1946) merely continued that trend. What differentiates the two periods is that the popular styles prevalent during the swing era were musically better than those of the 1920s, after years of influence from the jazzmen, while the hokiness was laid on even thicker. As a result, the best bands walked a continual artistic tightrope between good and bad taste, usually yielding to what the public preferred. In the long run, it was not so surprising that they occasionally lapsed, but rather that so much good music was created. Posterity must thank **Benny Goodman** (1909–1986) and his mentor, John Hammond, for many of the memorable successes.

Indeed, Goodman was a living legend for so long that one almost took for granted the amazing accomplishments of his long career. The band he first led in late 1934 and most of 1935 was somewhat lumpy and stodgy, especially in the rhythm section, and had only a few really good soloists. But as time went on, the great soloists came in, the band swung harder, and they entered the pages of history.

Goodman started his career as a kid of thirteen. He'd

stunned Bix Beiderbecke, who thought he was just a pest hanging around the bandstand, by playing some of the gutsiest and most imaginative clarinet Beiderbecke had ever heard. Others were pretty stunned, too, and by the ripe old age of eighteen Benny was a featured member of Ben Pollack's big band, where he doubled on cornet for brass section work. Here he made an impression on the New Yorkers as he played alongside Glenn Miller, Jimmy MacPartland, Gil Rodin, and Jack Teagarden. Goodman was picked up for several dates in the late 1920s and early 1930s with Red Nichols, Hoagy Carmichael, and Beiderbecke, and then, like so many others, disappeared under the swamp of the Depression.

Goodman's first band floundered stylistically until Fletcher Henderson's group disbanded in the fall of 1934. Prompted by jazz impresario John Hammond, Goodman hired Henderson as principal arranger, a fact that has since incurred the wrath of many a jazz critic. They would like to castigate Goodman for supposedly riding to success on Henderson's musical shoulders, suggesting that here was yet another whitey taking advantage of a black musician to make money for himself. However, Goodman constantly gave Henderson credit for having been instrumental in his success. Goodman freely admitted that, at least at first, his band couldn't play the arrangements as well as Henderson's had. He also paid Henderson well, certainly well enough to take him out of bankruptcy and make him solvent. When Henderson wanted to form another band of his own in 1935—one that Goodman knew would provide stiff musical competition—he let him go to do so. And when that last (and greatest) Henderson band failed, Goodman immediately hired him back. Clearly, there is not much of a case for Goodman's "exploitation" of Henderson.

Goodman set yet more trends in the music industry. He was the first bandleader to prominently feature a small combo, the Goodman Trio (and later Quartet). In that trio was pianist Teddy Wilson, the first black musician to play publicly with a white group. When Lionel Hampton was added on vibes, that made two; and after Lionel left to form *his* own band in 1940, along came guitarist Charlie Christian and trumpeter Cootie Williams.

As a player, Goodman was as aggressive yet rhapsodic on his instrument as Sidney Bechet was on the soprano sax. Unlike Bechet, he couldn't play within the New Orleans or bop idioms, but within his scope he was perfect. Goodman could (and did) drive whole sections with his clarinet, in addition to taking solos so inspiring that they forced his band members to new heights. There are many good albums of his work available, but the following two provide a fairly broad, concise overview of his career:

> *Benny Goodman's Greatest Hits*/Let's Dance; Clarinet à la King; Six Flats Unfurnished; Don't Be That Way; Jersey Bounce; Flying Home; Sing, Sing, Sing; Slipped Disc; Air Mail Special; Benny Rides Again; and Goodbye. Columbia PC/PCT-9283E (LP/Cs).

> *The Benny Goodman Story*/Let's Dance; Down South Camp Meeting; King Porter Stomp; It's Been So Long; Roll 'Em; Bugle Call Rag; Don't Be That Way; You Turned the Tables; Stompin' at the Savoy; Goody Goody; Slipped Disc; One O'Clock Jump; Memories of You; China Boy; Moonglow; Avalon; And the Angels Sing; Jersey Bounce; Shine; and Sing, Sing, Sing. MCA/MCAC-4055-2/MCAD-4055 (two LP/Cs, one CD).

The first album contains three selections by the great 1938–1939 band (including the Carnegie Hall version of "Don't Be That Way"), two arrangements by Eddie Sauter ("Clarinet à la King" and "Benny Rides Again"), and one by Richard Maltby ("Six Flats Unfurnished"). It also includes one recording by the 1939 Sextet, with Henderson on piano and Christian on guitar ("Flyin' Home"), and four cuts by Benny's 1960 ten-piece combo, which featured Red Norvo on vibes and Flip Phillips on tenor sax. The second album, while admittedly 1955 remakes, nevertheless reunites Goodman with many of his original stars: Harry James and Chris Griffin on trumpets, Murray McEachern on trombone, Hymie Schertzer and Babe Russin on saxes, Allan Reuss on guitar, and Gene Krupa on drums. Wilson is the pianist—not only in the trio, but with the big band, too; Hampton returns for two sparkling quartet performances ("Moonglow" and "Avalon"); and Martha Tilton performs her specialties, "You Turned the Tables on Me" and "And the Angels Sing." And through it all runs the golden thread of Goodman's clarinet.

While Goodman was "Stompin' at the Savoy," however, the house band there was already rocking the joint pretty well. This was the group led by drummer **Chick Webb** (1907–1939), one of the most underrated bands of all time, since it is better known for having "discovered" Ella Fitzgerald than for its own fine jazz. Little Chick, a hunchbacked dwarf whose feet could barely reach the bass drum pedal, was the first truly great *jazz* drummer (as opposed to great drummers who happened to play jazz). He provided an inspiring and sometimes spectacular beat that drove trumpeters Bobby Stark and Taft Jordan, saxists Pete Clark and Wayman Carver, trombonist Sandy Williams, and Ella on vocals. The following album, despite some cloying vocals, is outstanding:

> *Chick Webb 1935–1938*/Down Home Rag; I May Be Wrong; Facts and Figures; Go Harlem; There's Frost on the Moon; Rusty Hinge; Wake Up and Live; It's Swell of You; Clap Hands! Here Comes Charley; That Naughty Waltz; In a Little Spanish Town; I Got Rhythm; I Ain't Got Nobody; Strictly Jive; Sweet Sue; Squeeze Me; Harlem Congo; Midnite in a Madhouse; Azure; Spinnin' the Webb; Liza; Are You Here to Stay?; and Gee But You're Swell. Classics 517 (CD, avail. from Qualiton Records).

Webb's drums are underrecorded in the 1935 selections, but one can gauge the power and excitement of this band from "Down Home Rag" and "Facts and Figures"; Charles Linton, a saccharine vocalist, is heard on three titles as well.

While other big bands often had really awful-sounding vocal trios, Webb's soon featured Ella Fitzgerald and Armstrong-like trumpeter Taft Jordan, highlighting their considerable tone and swing ("Frost on the Moon" and "Wake Up and Live"). Also note the unusual "band-within-a-band," the Little Chicks, featuring clarinetist Chauncey Haughton in tandem with Wayman Carver, probably the first jazz flute soloist ("In a Little Spanish Town," "I Got Rhythm," and "Sweet Sue"). The sax solos of Edgar Sampson, the trombone of Sandy Williams, and the trumpets of Jordan and Stark are wonderful; but Webb is the star of the show, especially on "That Naughty Waltz," "Squeeze Me," "Harlem Congo," "Clap Hands!" and "Liza," which have even impressed such modern drummers as Elvin Jones.

Not letting Webb and Goodman get ahead of him, Duke Ellington entered his most consistently creative era during this period. If the years from 1927 to 1935 broke ground for Duke, those from 1936 to 1942 broke it twice over again. After adding bassist Jimmy Blanton and tenor saxist Ben Webster to his arsenal, it seemed there was no stopping him. Even the defection of Cootie Williams to Goodman's band in late 1940, a move that might have crippled a lesser leader, slowed him down only a little. Ellington brought in Ray Nance, a quadruple-threat talent (he sang and tap-danced in addition to playing exciting trumpet and violin) who created the famous solo on "Take the 'A' Train"—another of those solos that have been played virtually the same way ever since. The addition of **Billy Strayhorn** (1915–1967) as composer/arranger/relief pianist in 1941 only served to strengthen an already formidable lineup.

Two superb collections, one of them already cited, feature the richness of this period:

Ellington Era, Vol. 1/From this period: Clarinet Lament; Echoes of Harlem; In a Jam; Rose of the Rio Grande; Harmony in Harlem; Caravan; I Let a Song Go Out of

My Heart; Boy Meets Horn; Ridin' on a Bluenote; Jazz
Potpourri; Subtle Lament; Slap Happy; Portrait of the
Lion; The Gal From Joe's; Prelude to a Kiss; Stormy
Weather; Diminuendo and Crescendo in Blue; Sophisti-
cated Lady; The Sergeant Was Shy; Grievin'; and Battle
of Swing (Columbia, OP).

The Blanton-Webster Band/You, You Darlin'; Jack the Bear;
Ko-Ko; Morning Glory; Conga Brava; Concerto for Coo-
tie; Me and You; My Greatest Mistake; Cottontail; Never
No Lament; Dusk; Harlem Air Shaft; Bojangles; Portrait
of Bert Williams; Blue Goose; Rumpus in Richmond; All
Too Soon; Sepia Panorama; In a Mellotone; Five O'Clock
Whistle; Warm Valley; The Flaming Sword; Chloe; Across
the Tracks Blues; Sidewalks of New York; Take the "A"
Train; Are You Sticking?; Jumpin' Punkins; John Hardy's
Wife; Blue Serge; After All; Bakiff; Just A-Settin' and A-
Rockin'; I Got It Bad; The Giddybug Gallop; Chocolate
Shake; Clementine; Jump for Joy; Moon Over Cuba;
Flamingo; Five O'Clock Drag; Rocks in My Bed; Moon
Mist; Bli-Blip; Chelsea Bridge; Raincheck; I Don't Know
What Kind of Blues I Got; Perdido; C-Jam Blues; What
Am I Here For?; Johnny Come Lately; Main Stem; Hay-
foot, Strawfoot; Sentimental Lady; and Sherman Shuffle.
RCA 5659-1-RB/2-RB (four LPs/three CDs).

In addition to some superb solos—Nance's on " 'A' Train,"
Williams's on "Concerto for Cootie," Blanton's on "Jack the
Bear," Barney Bigard's on "Clarinet Lament," and Webster's
on "Cottontail"—it's the scoring that stars on these discs.
Particularly remarkable (from the late 1930s) are the disso-
nances of "Diminuendo and Crescendo in Blue," the strange
section of clarinet-alto sax-cornet-trombone on "Battle of
Swing," and the off-off-rhythms of "The Sergeant Was Shy."
In the early-'40s recordings, the subtler shadings—using a
big band as one would a small combo—helped keep Ellington
in the forefront of jazz orchestras. Especially interesting are
"Dusk," "Harlem Air Shaft," "Never No Lament," "Rumpus
in Richmond," "Jumpin' Punkins," "The Flaming Sword,"
"Chelsea Bridge," and "Raincheck."

The band that most jazz critics consider Duke's greatest

challenger was the one led by **Jimmie Lunceford** (1902–1947)—yet aside from a few early recordings (notably "Stratosphere" and "Rose Room"), the Lunceford style, for all its jazziness, tended toward the cute and overprecious. Indeed, in most of their famous recordings—"Baby, Won't You Please Come Home?" "For Dancers Only," and especially "Organ Grinder's Swing"—they play with an archness that does not stand up to repeated listening. The greatest talent of the Lunceford band turned out to be his principal arranger, **Sy Oliver** (1910–1988), who later achieved jazz greatness in Tommy Dorsey's band. On the album *Yes Indeed!* (RCA Bluebird 9987-2-RB), one can sample the ripe fruit of Oliver's loping, two-beat style in "Easy Does It," "Swanee River," "Yes Indeed!," "So What," and "Swingin' On Nothin'." His more aggressive style can be heard in "Quiet Please," "Opus #1" and the *sine qua non* of trumpet duels, "Well, Git It!," which features the incendiary high-note exploits of Chuck Peterson and **Ziggy Elman** (1914–1968), the latter one of the more colorful characters of the era, who came from the world of Yiddish klezmer music and blew out of the side of his mouth. These charts (and others) were played with more seriousness and greater fervor by Dorsey's band, collectively and individually, than Oliver had gotten from the Lunceford troops.

Indeed, Ellington was more challenged in this period by the orchestra led by "The Mad Mab," tenor and soprano saxist **Charlie Barnet** (1913–1991). Barnet, the black sheep of a wealthy New England family, had led a more conservative big band in 1936–1937; but in 1939 he threw caution to the wind and hired a wild crew of hell-raising jazzmen, whom he let loose on a slew of inspired arrangements by Bobby Burnet, Billy May, Andy Gibson, and himself. The result was a band with a slightly ragged, undisciplined ensemble, but a drive and collective color second to none. In fact, Barnet's arrangement of "Rockin' in Rhythm" was so much better than Ellington's that Duke rearranged the piece in 1943! The following album, therefore, is highly recommended:

Clap Hands, Here Comes Charlie/Knockin' at the Famous
Door; The Gal from Joe's; Cherokee; The Duke's Idea;
The Count's Idea; The Right Idea; Between 18th and 19th
on Chestnut Street; Clap Hands, Here Comes Charlie;
Leapin' at the Lincoln; Afternoon of a Moax; Flying
Home; Six Lessons from Madame La Zonga; Rockin' in
Rhythm; Pompton Turnpike; Wild Mab of the Fish Pond;
Redskin Rhumba; Southern Fried; Charleston Alley;
Lumby; and Murder at Peyton Hall. RCA Bluebird 6273-
1/2/4-RB (LP/CD/Cs).

Notice here the particularly loose and frenetic style per-
petrated by the Barnet crew and how, like Ellington, the
leader's playing permeates the proceedings. In this case, however, the instrument is tenor sax (and sometimes soprano)
rather than piano, and that difference makes for a group
that jumps like a Coleman Hawkins solo rather than bouncing
lightly.

Ellington's other great competitor was the band led by
William "Count" Basie (1905–1984). Basie, originally from
New Jersey but stranded in Kansas City in 1928 (as the result
of a touring band that went bankrupt), had been a featured
soloist on Bennie Moten's great band (see Chapter 3). When
Moten died in 1935, his brother Bus took over for a while,
but later disbanded the group. Basie picked up some of the
best talent, filled in with some locals, and began playing (and
broadcasting) around town. They came to the attention of
jazz impresario John Hammond, who brought them to New
York, where they changed some of the personnel and landed
recording contracts with Decca and Columbia.

Basie's band developed the riff to a form of high art. The
leader himself spearheaded an economical piano style that
became his trademark and that was copied by endless pianists
throughout the 1930s and 1940s. More than that, however,
the driving rhythm section of guitarist Freddie Green and
bassist Walter Page, the light, airy, cymbal-accented drums
of Jo Jones, and the harmonically daring trumpet solos of
Buck Clayton (1911–), and the breathy, liquid tenor sax of
Lester "Prez" Young (1909–1959) all helped greatly to bring

about the birth of bebop six to eight years later. The following albums, then, are very worthwhile:

> *Count Basie: One O'Clock Jump*/Honeysuckle Rose; Pennies from Heaven; Swinging at the Daisy Chain; Roseland Shuffle; Exactly Like You; Boo Hoo; The Glory of Love; Boogie Woogie; Smarty; Listen My Children; One O'Clock Jump; John's Idea; Good Morning Blues (two tks.); Our Love Was Meant to Be; Time Out; and Topsy. MCA/MCAC/MCAD-42324 (LP/CD/Cs).

> *The Essential Count Basie, Vol. 2*/I Can't Believe That You're in Love With Me; Clap Hands, Here Comes Charlie; Dickie's Dream; Lester Leaps In; The Apple Jump; I Left My Baby; Volcano; Between the Devil and the Deep Blue Sea; I Never Knew; Tickle Toe; Louisiana; Easy Does It; Let Me See; Blow Top; Gone With "What" Wind; and Super Chief. CBS CJ/CK/CJT-40835 (LP/CD/Cs).

Young's contributions may best be judged by his intro on "Time Out," his solo on "One O'Clock Jump," and the small-group sides, "Dickie's Dream" and "Lester Leaps In." His harmonic daring was as much admired as his style, which eliminated bar lines in even the most frenetic passages. On the downside, his tenor tone was pallid and bland, often going in one ear and out the other. One must listen carefully to catch all of Young's harmonic-melodic innovations, or else they go right by. In addition to the above-named soloists, one must also point out the wonderfully driving, urban-bluesy vocals of **Jimmy Rushing** (1903–1972), the rich-toned tenor sax of Herschel Evans, the spirited trumpet breaks of Harry "Sweets" Edison, the occasional presence of Eddie Durham (the first electric guitarist in jazz), and last (but not least) the trombone playing of **Dicky Wells** (1909–1986). Wells's flat, cool tone, sighing style in ballads and remarkable lip and slide dexterity marked the first and most influential advance in the instrument since Harrison and Teagarden came along in the 1920s. Indeed, Wells slid easily in the same circles as bop giants Charlie Parker and Dizzy Gillespie, not to mention influencing the great J. J. Johnson; but that will be addressed in the next chapter.

Jimmy Rushing's female counterpart in the Basie vocal section was, for the most part, a good singer named Helen Humes. But for a period of eight months, he also featured one of the greatest jazz/blues singers of all time, **Billie Holiday** (1915–1959). She'd made a few obscure sides in 1933, but it was this stint with Basie that really brought her to prominence. She sang for a time with the band of Artie Shaw and recorded with Paul Whiteman before embarking on a successful solo career. Because she was signed to Columbia-Vocalion while the Basie band was with Decca, making records with the full band was impossible, but Basie sidemen accompanied her on several fine discs, and air checks exist of Holiday and Basie to let listeners know what all the fuss was about.

Billie Holiday had a wiry, acidic voice that she knew how to use to express pain and suffering. She could "bend" notes like a master horn player, her timing was (in those days) impeccable, and her influence on a whole generation of singers—Ella Fitzgerald included—was enormous. She also developed a special working relationship with Lester "Prez" Young, who continued to accompany her on records and club dates long after both of them had left the Basie fold. Indeed, some of Young's best playing was as an obbligato horn to Holiday. The following album, which covers 1933–1939, is superb in every way:

The Billie Holiday Story, Vol. 1/Your Mother's Son-In-Law; Did I Remember; Riffin' the Scotch; Them There Eyes; These Foolish Things; No Regrets; A Fine Romance; Easy to Love; The Way You Look Tonight; I Can't Give You Anything But Love; This Year's Kisses; Pennies From Heaven; That's Life, I Guess; I'll Never Be the Same; Why Was I Born?; Without Your Love; Getting Some Fun Out of Life; Swing, Brother, Swing!; They Can't Take That Away From Me; I Can't Get Started; On the Sentimental

Side; Travlin' All Alone; When You're Sailing; If Dreams Come True; You Go to My Head; Back in Your Own Back Yard; When a Woman Loves a Man; The Very Thought of You; and four others. Columbia PG-32121 (two LPs).

In addition to the Basie crew, which is heard on "Swing, Brother, Swing!," "They Can't Take That Away From Me," and "I Can't Get Started," the above discs also feature trumpeters Hot Lips Page, Charlie Shavers, Jonah Jones, and Shirley Clay; trombonists Teagarden and Tyree Glenn; clarinetists Goodman and Artie Shaw; drummers Krupa and Cozy Cole; and pianist Teddy Wilson, another of her very special friends.

One of Basie's best competitors in Kansas City was bandleader **Andy Kirk** (1898–), whose Twelve Clouds of Joy made some particularly joyous music. The best Cloud of all, though, was pianist **Mary Lou Williams** (1909–1982), whose rocking solos and musically subtle arrangements helped set the band's tone and shape its style. When she left in 1942, most of the band's personality and identity went with her. Curiously, she refused to start a band of her own, retreating to trio work and, eventually, leaving jazz entirely. This album, however, assures her a place in jazz history:

Instrumentally Speaking/Walkin' and Swingin'; Moten Swing; Big Jim Blues; Lotta Sax Appeal; Git; Froggy Bottom; Mary's Idea; Steppin' Pretty; Wednesday Night Hop; In the Groove; Floyd's Guitar Blues; Ring Dem Bells; Boogie Woogie Cocktail; and McGhee Special. MCA/MCAC-1308 (LP/Cs).

At least six of the above are Williams compositions, as are eleven of the arrangements. The last two tracks are the band's best after she left. "McGhee Special" features an astounding tour de force by rising young trumpet star Howard McGhee, but still the Clouds of Joy without Mary Lou Williams just wasn't the same attraction. To this day, some people feel the band was really a co-op, that the easygoing Kirk only fronted it to procure better bookings. He continued to lead it six more unfruitful years without Williams, so the real story is anyone's guess.

One of the least-remembered yet (paradoxically) greatest bands of the era was Earl Hines's Grand Terrace Orchestra of 1938–1942. It was stocked with superb players such as trumpeters Walter Fuller, tenor saxist Budd Johnson, clarinetist Omer Simeon (who had been an important member of Morton's Red Hot Peppers), and drummer **Alvin Burroughs** (1911–1950), one of the swing era's unsung heroes. Indeed, Burroughs's beat was so lithe, so crisp and propulsive, riding on the cymbal and snare in a way that presaged the bop drummers, that "swing" was hardly the term for it; "glide" would have been more apropos.

Curiously, however, Hines's own piano was rarely featured in those years, and when it was, it sounded like that of any other stride stylist of the era, played in an undistinguished manner. Fortunately, Hines was able to make some solo recordings during this period (the first four listed below are examples) that showed his keyboard mastery had not dimmed:

> *Earl Hines: Piano Man*/Rosetta; Child of a Disordered Brain; On the Sunny Side of the Street; Melancholy Baby; Piano Man; Blues in Thirds; Riff Medley; Grand Terrace Shuffle; Boogie Woogie on St. Louis Blues; Father Steps In; Number 19; Tantalizing a Cuban; Jelly, Jelly; Second Balcony Jump; Stormy Monday Blues; and The Father Jumps. RCA Bluebird 6750-1/2/4-RB (LP/CD/Cs).

In addition to the soloists mentioned, it's important to note the blues styling of Billy Eckstine ("Jelly, Jelly"), which completely revolutionized the art of blues singing with a big band and was to influence vocalists such as Joe Williams. When Burroughs left the band in 1941, Hines managed to find a good replacement in the equally unknown Rudy Traylor.

However, their lack of commercial success spelled doom for the band, which reached its artistic zenith in 1943 (during a recording ban, organized by the Musicians' Union to protest salaries and royalties), when it included both Charlie Parker and Dizzy Gillespie.

Also present during the early 1940s was Benny Carter, fresh from his triumphs in Europe and as interesting as ever. His unique style of scoring saxes, which promoted a feather-weight, dancing beat, was redoubled in his big band by former Ellington bassist Hayes Alvis and drummer William Purnell, one of the few blacks to pursue the deftly swinging style of Dave Tough. In addition, the band also featured such outstanding soloists as trumpeters Bill Coleman and Shad Collins, trombonist Sandy Williams (a refugee from the by then broken band of Chick Webb), and Carter himself, who played clarinet and alto sax. They can all be heard, along with Carter's composing and arranging abilities, in such cuts as "Scandal in A Flat," "When Lights Are Low," "Slow Freight," "I Surrender Dear," "Smack," "Riff Romp," and "Vagabond Dreams" on *Benny Carter and his Orchestra 1939–1940*, Classics 579 (Qualiton Imports).

Two of the most unusual big bands, however, were those led by trumpeter **Erskine Hawkins** (1914–) and pop crooner **Bob Crosby** (1913–), outfits that were as different from each other as they were from the remainder of the big-band fold. Hawkins, who bore the nickname "The 20th-Century Gabriel" when his band followed Chick Webb's into the Savoy Ballroom, was a lyrical player who stuck close to the melody while exploiting the trumpet's high range in a way that prefaced the work of Willie "Cat" Anderson in the 1940s and 1950s. His band, which had come up North from Alabama, explored the transference of the blues from its rural southern vocal style to the slick arrangements of a swing-era band. Hawkins accomplished this by assigning the "vocal" line to his own trumpet, which would play the melody, after which the soloists and ensemble would "take off" with some exquisite, moody scores. His rhythm section bore a striking resemblance to that of Earl Hines's band, which was undoubtedly one of his role models, yet the "southern style" was never absent from its playing:

> *The Original Tuxedo Junction*/Tuxedo Junction; After Hours; Tippin' In; Rockin' Rollers' Jubilee; Weary Blues; Easy Rider; Swing Out; Swingin' on Lenox Avenue; Gin Mill Special; Cherry; Dolomite; Junction Blues; Sweet Georgia Brown; Soft Winds; Nona; Blackout; Don't Cry, Baby; and Bear Mash Blues. RCA Bluebird 9682-1/2/4-RB (LP/CD/Cs).

Hawkins's outstanding soloists included trumpeter Wilbur "Dud" Bascomb, alto saxist Bill Johnson, tenor saxist Julian Dash, and pianist Avery Parrish. All were fine, original players—indeed, Dizzy Gillespie has often credited Dud Bascomb as one of his strongest early influences (next to Roy Eldridge, of course). Big-band aficionados will notice the presence here of "Tuxedo Junction," associated in the public mind with the popular band of Glenn Miller, but it was Hawkins and Dash who co-wrote the tune. This was the first recording (a year before Miller), and the song became the band's theme.

Bob Crosby, Bing's younger brother, was selected as the "front man" by a group of New Orleans- and Chicago-style musicians who were refugees from Ben Pollack's orchestra. The actual leader of the band, behind the scenes, was saxist/arranger **Gil Rodin** (1906–1974), who picked the musicians, selected the repertoire, and conducted rehearsals. The foundation of the band was the solid beat laid down by drummer Ray Bauduc (pronounced Bah-*dook*) and bassist Bob Haggart, who produced the popular bass-drum duet "Big Noise from Winnetka." The other Crosby stars were trumpeter Yank Lawson, tenor saxist Eddie Miller, clarinetist/arranger Matty Matlock, saxist/arranger Dean Kincaide, and pianists Joe Sullivan and Bob Zurke of the Chicago barrelhouse school.

These freewheeling musicians, who were all born at about the same time (betwen 1907 and 1911), developed an affinity for one another's playing unusual in the ever-changing world of big-band personnel.

In the beginning, their repertoire was old-fashioned by the standards of the day, and in a sense a precursor of the "Moldy Fig" revival of the early 1940s. Before long, however, they developed their own original numbers, which included Sullivan's "Little Rock Getaway" (played on the record by Zurke because Sullivan was drunk) and their biggest all-time hit, "South Rampart Street Parade." The latter, in fact, has become so much of a "Dixieland" standard that most of those who play it are unaware that it is *not* an authentic New Orleans marching tune! By 1939, however, the band was relying less and less on the big-band Chicago-Dixie style that had propelled them to fame, and eventually veered toward a more standard New York–style sound created by swing arranger Jimmy Mundy. The Crosby band lost its identifying sound, and with it its audience, but the following album shows what all the fuss was about:

> *South Rampart Street Parade*/Dixieland Shuffle; Royal Garden Blues; The Old Spinning Wheel; Between the Devil and the Deep Blue Sea; Little Rock Getaway; South Rampart Street Parade; Dogtown Blues; Panama; Wolverine Blues; Big Noise from Winnetka; Swingin' at the Sugar Bowl; I'm Prayin' Humble; What's New?; My Inspiration; Skater's Waltz; Air Mail Stomp; Complainin'; Jimtown Blues; Milenberg Joys; and Chain Gang. GRP/Decca GRD-615 (CD).

One of the most unusual soloists, composers, or bandleaders of the era was xylophonist/marimba player (and later vibist) **Red Norvo** (1905–). His forte was not heat but a cool sound, one he had learned from his friend Bix Beiderbecke. While other bands were evidently trying to tear the roof off, Norvo's was lithe, supple, and subtle. One of the chief contributors to the Norvo sound was arranger **Eddie Sauter**

(1914–), before he went to Goodman; another was Norvo's wife, singer **Mildred Bailey** (1907–1951), the first great white female jazz vocalist. Like Norvo, her strength was subtlety and shading rather than belting. As a result, they made a wonderful artistic duo, even as their personal life together was marred by Mildred's neuroses. The following album, therefore, is highly recommended:

> *Red Norvo Featuring Mildred Bailey*/Knockin' on Wood; Hole in the Wall; In a Mist; Dance of the Octopus; Old-Fashioned Love; I Surrender, Dear; Tom Boy; The Night Is Blue; Honeysuckle Rose; With All My Heart and Soul; Bug House; Blues in E-Flat; A Porter's Love Song to a Chambermaid; Remember; I Let a Song Go Out of My Heart; and Just You, Just Me. Portrait Masters RK-44118 (CD).

Though only the last four selections feature the Norvo big band, they all serve to highlight a specific aspect of his talent, whether in the free-for-all jam sessions of "Honeysuckle Rose" and "Bug House" or the particularly avant-garde small ensembles of "Hole in the Wall" or Norvo's masterpiece, "Dance of the Octopus," a free-form, loosely structured exploration of color and harmonic daring unsurpassed in its day (1933). Norvo's only flaw as a jazz soloist was a certain inhibition to swing. Even though his sense of rhythm was impeccable, there always seemed to be a sort of pulling back even when what was called for was a pushing forward.

Speaking of great soloists, one of the greatest was getting his act together. Louis Armstrong, after a period of wayward abandon, had finally hurt his lip by going for so many high C's. He was out of action for nearly a year. When he came back, it was to reveal a new style in which all the elements of the old had congealed into one perfect whole. Those who like antiquities may never admit it, but the years from 1936 to 1942 were among Armstrong's greatest. His playing still had the drive and joy of old, but the wild abandon was replaced by a new composure. He reached inward rather than outward, and what he found were moments of beauty unparalleled at that time. The following LP is proof enough:

> *Louis Armstrong 4: Swing That Music* (OP)/Lyin' to Myself; Ev'n-tide; Swing That Music; Thankful; The Skeleton in the Closet; Mahogany Hall Stomp; When the Saints Go Marchin' In; Yours and Mine; Dippermouth Blues; Public Melody Number One; It's Wonderful; I Double Dare You; and Struttin' With Some Barbecue. MCA/MCAC-1312 (LP/Cs).

The swing era had one very positive effect on Armstrong: It made him get a band that swung instead of slushing behind him. True, he went back in time to pull out such old-timers as bassist Pops Foster and drummer Paul Barbarin, and Luis Russell was still musical director, but at least the saxes played legit, instead of Lombardo-styled moaning. With time he gained such strong players as clarinetist Albert Nicholas and trumpeters Henry "Red" Allen and Shelton Hemphill. "Skeleton" and "Dippermouth" feature the Jimmy Dorsey big band, where he had the advantage of being backed by drummer Ray McKinley, but in this period Armstrong was so great that few could compete with him.

One of those few was **Roy Eldridge** (1911–1989), a great transitional figure in trumpet history. He can be heard, on the Fletcher Henderson set, in such excellent settings as the famed "Christopher Columbus." One hears a player with a tone a little less full and rich than Armstrong's, but with just as much endurance and an even greater technique. It is to Eldridge that we trace the start of the "speed" trumpeter—he was so fast that fellow players were literally scared off the stand when he sat in.

What made Eldridge's style so commanding, influential, and scary was the fact that speed wasn't all he had to offer. Early in his career, circa 1931, he was heard by Chick Webb, who said, "Yeah, you're fast, but you ain't sayin' nothin'. Go check out Louis, then come back and let me hear you." Eventually, enough people said it so that Eldridge listened. He made a concerted effort to play more coherent solos, and by 1935 he was really *ready*. After stints with the big bands of Teddy Hill and Henderson, he began his own group. They played in Chicago and featured such good players as alto saxist Scoops Carey and drummer Zutty Singleton. They built a reputation but little money. Then Eldridge did some studio dates, backing Billie Holiday and Mildred Bailey. When Gene Krupa left Goodman to form his own band, he made several offers to Eldridge to join. Eldridge kept saying no, but in 1941 he agreed. He stayed a few years, left, and came back in the late 1940s before embarking on a solo career. The following albums sum up his pre-1950 style:

> *Little Jazz*/Here Comes Cookie; When I Grow Too Old to Dream; Christopher Columbus; Big Chief De Sota; Blue Lou; Stealin' Apples; Mary Had a Little Lamb; Too Good to Be True; Warmin' Up; Blues in C Sharp Minor; Wabash Stomp (two tks.); Florida Stomp; Heckler's Hop; Where the Lazy River Goes By; That Thing; After You've Gone; Wham; Fallin' in Love Again; and I'm Nobody's Baby. CBS CJ/CK/CJT-45275 (LP/CD/Cs).

> *Uptown (w/Gene Krupa & Anita O'Day)*/Green Eyes; Let Me Off Uptown; Kick It!; After You've Gone; Rockin' Chair; Amour; Stop! The Red Light's On; Watch the Birdie; The Walls Keep Talking; Skylark; Bolero at the Savoy; Thanks for the Boogie Ride; Keep 'Em Flying; Pass the Bounce; Ball of Fire; Harlem on Parade; Knock Me a Kiss; Barrelhouse Bessie From Basin Steet; That Drummer's Band; Murder He Says; Bop Boogie; Watch Out; Swiss Lullaby; and Why Fall in Love With a Stranger? CBS CK/CJT-45448 (CD/Cs).

Most of the material here is breathtaking, but the real winners are take two of "Wabash Stomp" and the Krupa version of "After You've Gone," plus the recordings of "Heckler's Hop," "Warmin' Up," "That Thing," "Amour," "Rockin' Chair," and "Swiss Lullaby." In the *Uptown* album, we hear a rarity within the entertainment framework of the swing era: the coming together in one band of three outstanding jazz talents. By 1941, Krupa and Eldridge were known entities, but the singing of **Anita O'Day** (1919–) was something entirely new and radical for its time: a very hip, completely *jazz* approach to female band vocals. Despite offstage apathy toward each other, Anita O'Day and Roy Eldridge complemented each other musically, in their urban hipness, the way Lester Young complemented Billie Holiday.

Another spectacular soloist—as far as spectacularity goes, probably the utmost—was vibist/pianist/drummer/dancer **Lionel Hampton** (1909–). We've already discussed him in relation to Goodman's quartet, but he is chiefly known as a soloist. During his years with Goodman (1937–1941), Hampton was contracted by Victor to make records of jam sessions for them. The result was no less than ninety-five existing masters, assembled in 1976 as a six-LP set, and recently issued on four separate CDs. This will be the largest series of recommended recordings by any one artist in this book. But since the jam session was (and remains) an integral part of jazz, and since these discs have in the main a completely uninhibited feel and feature most of the greats of the era, it's worthwhile to list the entire set:

Lionel Hampton, 1937–1941/My Last Affair; Jivin' the Vibres; The Mood That I'm In; Hampton Stomp; Whoa, Babe; Buzzin' Around With the Bee; I Know That You Know; Stompology; I'm Confessin'; On the Sunny Side of the Street; Rhythm Rhythm; China Stomp; Drum Stomp; Piano Stomp; I Surrender, Dear; The Object of My Affection; Judy; Baby, Won't You Please Come Home?; Everybody Loves My Baby; After You've Gone; You're My Ideal; The Sun Will Shine Tonight; Ring Dem Bells; Don't Be That Way; Shoe Shiner's Drag; I'm in the Mood for Swing; Any Time at All; High Society; Muskrat Ramble; Rock Hill Special; Down Home Jump; Fiddle Diddle; I Can Give You Love; It Don't Mean a Thing; Big Wig in the Wigwam; Johnny Get Your Horn; Shufflin' at the Hollywood (two tks); Sweethearts on Parade: I Just Couldn't Take It, Baby; Denison Swing; Wizzin' the Wiz;

Ain'tcha Comin' Home; My Buddy; Stand By! For Further Announcements; Memories of You; If It's Good; 12th Street Rag; The Jumpin' Jive; One Sweet Letter From You; When Lights Are Low (two tks); Hot Mallets; Early Session Hop; I'm on My Way Home from You; Haven't Named It Yet; I Can't Get Started; Hebbie Jeebies (two tks); Munson St. Breakdown; I've Found a New Baby: Four or Five Times; Gin for Christmas; Dinah (two tks); Till Tom Special; Singin' the Blues; Flying Home; Save It, Pretty Mama; Shades of Jade; Tempo and Swing; House of Morgan; I'd Be Lost Without You; Central Ave. Breakdown; Jack the Bellboy; Dough-Rey-Mi; Jivin' with Jarvis; Blue; Just for Laffs; Ghost of a Chance; Martin on Every Block; Pig Foot Sonata; Lost Love; Charlie Was a Sailor; Attitude; Bogo Joe; Open House; Give Me Some Skin; Smart Aleck; and five others. Classics 524 (Vol. 1), 534 (Vol. 2), 562 (Vol. 3), 624 (Vol. 4) (CDs, available from Qualiton Imports).

Included in this absolutely mind-blowing set are trumpeters Rex Stewart, Ziggy Elman, Cootie Williams, Red Allen, Jonah Jones, Harry James, and Dizzy Gillespie; trombonists Lawrence Brown and J. C. Higginbotham; clarinetists Buster Bailey, Vido Musso, Edmond Hall, and Marshall Royal; saxists Hymie Schertzer, Herschel Evans, Johnny Hodges, Benny Carter, Russell Procope, Chu Berry, Harry Carney, Coleman Hawkins, Toots Mondello, Ben Webster, and Earl Bostic; pianists Billy Kyle, Jess Stacy, Clyde Hart, Nat "King" Cole, Joe Sullivan, and Sir Charles Thompson; bassists John Kirby, Billy Taylor, Milt Hinton, and Artie Bernstein; guitarist Charlie Christian; drummers Gene Krupa, Cozy Cole, Sonny Greer, Jo Jones, Sid Catlett, Zutty Singleton, and Kaiser Marshall; and the entire Earl Hines big band (minus Hines himself), including Fuller, Simeon, Budd Johnson, and Burroughs. This practically encyclopedic gathering of the greats or greats-to-be of the era, in an informal music-making situation, makes this by far the single finest collection of swing music (or just plain *jazz* music) ever assembled under the name of one man. It should also be noted that though the six-LP set listed above is out of print, RCA has reissued a little more than a third of it on two albums: *Hot Mallets* (RCA Bluebird 6458-1/2/4-RB, LP/CD/Cs) and *The Jumpin' Jive* (RCA 2433-1/2/4-RB, LP/CD/Cs). Still, the original, complete package is preferable.

Undoubtedly, however, the most compelling popular fad of the 1930s, which was also a jazz fad, was the sudden resurgence of boogie-woogie. As discussed in Chapter 2, this style was popularized among Chicago musicians by Pine Top Smith, but it had its roots in the rural southern blues, and indeed generally clung to the twelve-bar format. During the late 1930s, one of the actual creators of this style, pianist **Jimmy Yancey** (1894–1951), benefited briefly from the boogie craze. Yancey's style was unlike any other boogie pianist's, utilizing a loping, single-note "walking" bass in the left hand rather than the more popular (and famous) eight-to-the-bar chord pounding as popularized by Pete Johnson and Albert Ammons. Yancey's blues-drenched improvisations made an interesting contrast to their style in the following album, which also features a soloist of in-between talent, **Meade "Lux" Lewis** (1905–1964), whose playing was not as loose as Yancey's, while at the same time not as simple or restrictive as Johnson's and Ammons's:

> *Barrelhouse Boogie/Meade "Lux" Lewis*: Honkey Tonk Train Blues; and Whistlin' Blues. *Jimmy Yancey*: Yancey Stomp; State Street Special; Tell 'Em About Me; Five O'Clock Blues; Slow and Easy Blues; The Mellow Blues; Crying in My Sleep; Death Letter Blues; Yancey's Bugle Call; and 35th and Dearborn. *Peter Johnson and Albert Ammons*: Boogie Woogie Man; Boogie Woogie Jump; Barrelhouse Boogie; Cuttin' the Boogie; Foot Pedal Boogie; Walkin' the Boogie; Sixth Avenue Express; Pine Creek; and Movin' the Boogie. RCA Bluebird 8334-1/2/4-RB (LP/CD/Cs).

One can tell the difference in styles by their effect on the listener: Lewis and Yancey leave you wanting to hear more, while the Johnson-Ammons duo sounds like déjà vu after just four cuts. The boogie piano fad died out by 1942, leaving most of these players out of work (though Lewis moved to Blue Note, where he remained until 1944). It was a simple yet infectious style that found its realization in rhythm-and-blues music rather than affecting the jazz mainstream.

Before leaving the era, we have one more soloist and one more band to discuss. First is the amazing progress made by Coleman Hawkins in becoming the preeminent tenor saxist of the era. Hawkins wasn't the fastest player around, but his huge tone and the soul he put into his music made him a giant. We've already examined him, in the recordings with Henderson, but now we'll take him a little further on.

After leaving Henderson, Hawk spent five years in Europe (samples of his work with Django Reinhardt are on Prestige 7633), during which he consolidated his tone and technique to dominate the scene. When he returned to the United States, he formed a small swing band whose biggest hit was "Body and Soul." This disc was a landmark in that it broke into the "pop" market without pandering in the least to any swing-era formula. In fact, except for the first few notes, Hawkins never does play the melody at all. What's more, as the later selections on this album prove, he continued to evolve his style through the 1940s and 1950s, adapting (like Sidney Bechet) to play with such boppers as Fats Navarro, J. J. Johnson, and Max Roach, plus creating a unique ballad style:

> *Body and Soul*/Meet Dr. Foo; Fine Dinner; She's Funny That Way; Body and Soul (two vers.); When Day Is Done; Sheik of Araby; I Love You; My Blue Heaven; Bouncing with Bean; How Strange; Half Step Down, Please; April in Paris; Angel Face; Jumping for Jane; There Will Never Be Another You; Little Girl Blue; His Very Own Blues; Dinner for One, Please, James; 39"-25"-39"; Have You Met Miss Jones?; and The Bean Stalks Again. RCA Bluebird 5658-1/4-RB, 5717-2-RB (two LPs/Cs, one CD).

The last *group* we have to discuss is another of those like the 1926–1929 Five Pennies. Unlike them, however, they lasted longer, were more cohesive, and influenced many groups to come. This was the **John Kirby Sextet**, one of the few groups in jazz history led by a bass player. They were known in their heyday as The Biggest Little Band in the Land, and they earned that title honestly.

They started out rather informally in 1937, with Frankie Newton on trumpet and Pete Brown on alto sax, but after a few personnel changes they came up with a truly winning combination. In their peak years they consisted of trumpeter **Charlie Shavers** (1919–1971), who was nineteen when he joined Kirby in 1938; Russell Procope, a veteran of the Morton and Henderson bands, on alto; Buster Bailey, a classically trained clarinetist from Chicago who'd played with King Oliver; pianist Billy Kyle, a highly underrated musician who later played with Armstrong; Kirby, another Henderson alumnus, on bass; and O'Neil Spencer, a quiet, unostentatious man, on drums. Their 1938–1942 recordings remain masterpieces of their kind: a fleet, tight, skimming kind of swing in which each soloist picked up where the other left off, embellishing in perpetual motion rather than in spurts. Their arrangements were highly imaginative, providing an almost classical balance to music normally associated with loud jamming. Indeed, as some of their record titles indicate, they had some reworked classics in their repertoire:

> *The Biggest Little Band*/Afternoon in Africa; Dizzy Debutante; I Love You Truly; Planter's Punch; Sloe Jam Fizz; Rehearsin' for a Nervous Breakdown; From A Flat to C; Pastel Blue; Undecided; Chained to a Dream; Light Up; It Feels Good; Drink to Me Only With Thine Eyes; Sweet Georgia Brown (two tks.); Front and Center; Opus 5; Jumpin' in the Pump Room; Blue Skies; Serenade; Blues Petite; 20th Century Closet; Royal Garden Blues; Pinetop's Boogie Woogie; Eccentric Rag; Chloe; Andiology; Can't We Be Friends?; Coquette; Beethoven Riffs On; Zooming at the Zombie; and Cuttin' the Campus. Smithsonian P2-14584 (two LPs).

In the above collection, one can hear their many strengths and few weaknesses. Some critics dismiss them as a jazz group because of their tendency to overrefine their playing and because their pop treatment of classics resulted in pastiches that cannot be easily classified as classical or jazz. We also hear, as in "Pinetop's Boogie Woogie," how they occasionally stiffened up on jazz accents; and how, in "Blue Skies," some of their arrangements leaned toward a Muzak treatment.

Conversely, they produced a good deal of great music. Works such as "Opus 5," "Jumpin' in the Pump Room," and "Rehearsin' for a Nervous Breakdown" followed unusual harmonic and rhythmic changes. In "From A Flat to C,'" they swing through the harmonic cycle of fifths with an audacity rare even today. Their version of "Sweet Georgia Brown" barely touches the melody, except in Shavers's trumpet solo, and their reworking of New Orleans chestnuts such as "Royal Garden" and "Eccentric" are truly marvelous. In short, this was a group whose enormous popularity and slight tendency toward preciousness garnered sneers from contemporary (and later) jazz critics. However, in the decades since they disbanded, their work sounds more modern for its time with each passing year.

5.
Changing Tides

Throughout the entire swing era, there remained a small but hard-core group of jazz fans so traditional that to them even Jelly Roll Morton sounded modern. To these listeners, any group larger than seven pieces was monstrous, anything arranged for longer than eight bars pompous and heretical. They wanted to bring back King Oliver, but he inconveniently died on them in 1938. Much to their delight, the ODJB reunited in 1936, but they, too, were gone again by 1938. Armstrong and Bechet were still around, of course, but their playing was getting too "modern" for them. So they found Bunk Johnson, bought him a trumpet and a new set of false teeth to play it with, and brought him to the Big Apple in the early 1940s.

Since hearing original players was getting harder and harder to do because of advancing age and changing styles, a group of young white musicians in California decided to form their own New Orleans-style combo. This was the Yuerba Buena Jazz Band, led by trumpeter **Lu Watters** (1911–1990). Back came the banjos and tubas, and with them a pretty poor simulation of the Creole Jazz Band, but Watters and his group spurred a whole new movement of traditionalists, unkindly known to the circle of more progressive jazzmen as the Moldy Figs.

The Moldy Fig movement was just as dead-ended as the white Chicago style of the 1920s, but at least the Chicagoans were at one time originals. Watters and his successor, cornetist **Bob Scobey** (1916–), were nothing more than imitators of a style already dead and gone. As time went by, some of these groups provided a real service by faithfully re-creating original Morton, Redman, and Bill Challis scores for generations that had never heard them. By and large, however, the flock of traditional bands that grew out of Watters's passion for the past were, like his, stiff, corny, and derivative.

Meanwhile, a new movement was afoot within the swing set. Primary among these, insofar as small groups were concerned, was the remarkable trio led by pianist-singer **Nat "King" Cole** (1919–1965), whose impact on jazz was vastly underrated because of his later commercial success as a pop ballad singer. It's important to recall that in the early-to-mid-1940s, Cole completely revolutionized the concept of jazz piano, in a sense creating a style that was the antithesis of such keyboard virtuosos as Johnson, Hines, and Tatum. In effect, Cole broke down each phrase to its barest components and substituted new rhythms and startling new harmonies, sometimes using descending chromatics and utilizing the melody line as a ninth or eleventh chord above them.

Helping greatly in the creative process was guitarist **Oscar Moore**, another underrated player, whose ear for harmonics and bright, gutsy alteration of quick chording and single-note playing represented a continuation of the Reinhardt-Christian approach. At times Cole and Moore played together in dizzyingly rapid single-note phrases, a modern counterpart to the playing in thirds done in the early 1920s by Oliver and Armstrong, while Cole's powerful left hand and the walking bass of Johnny Miller (who replaced the original bassist, Wesley Prince) led them to dispense entirely with drums. This new form of a "drummerless" band brought objections from club owners at first, but Cole's sympathetic rapport with his audiences, his smile, and most especially the warm, ingratiating sound of his voice, whether speaking or singing, eventually won the plaudits of critics and casual listeners alike. "I knew all along that I knew what I was doing," Cole said years later. "Once the club owners agreed with me, it was plain sailing."

Cole's singing should also not be taken lightly. Though he generally stuck close to the melody and shunned scatting, his rhythmic style was unique and innovative, sometimes anticipating the beat but more often riding across it, creating a tension between the nervous trickle of his pianism and the relaxed swing of the voice. In addition, his new, vibratoless sound greatly influenced such later stylists as Mel Tormé, Dave Lambert, and Jon Hendricks, notwithstanding their pursuit of scatting. In other words, Nat Cole almost single-handedly paved the way for the next generation of pianists and singers, as the following 1943–1950 recordings amply demonstrate:

Jumpin' at Capitol: The Best of the Nat King Cole Trio/Jumpin' at Capitol; Straighten Up and Fly Right; Gee, Baby, Ain't I Good to You?; Sweet Lorraine; It's Only a Paper Moon; When I Take My Sugar to Tea; The Frim Fram Sauce; I'm a Shy Guy; Embraceable You; (I Love You) For Sentimental Reasons; What Is This Thing Called Love?; Come To, Baby Do; All for You; Route 66; If You Can't Smile and Say Yes; and For You, My Love. Rhino Records R21S/R41H-71009 (CD/Cs, available from Rhino Records, Dept. C-11d, 2225 Colorado Ave., Santa Monica, CA 90404-3555).

The type of rhythmic and harmonic innovations that the King Cole Trio had been employing since 1939 also began to affect the orchestral scene as well. In 1943, a new kind of big band broke on the scene, whose sound was immediately loved or hated by its listeners. This was the orchestra led by **Stan Kenton** (1912–1979), a pianist and arranger from Balboa Beach, California. Kenton's band, unlike any others then, didn't play for dancing; their beat was too complex, their tempos often changed in the midst of a piece, and the wild-

JELLY ROLL MORTON

LEON RAPPOLO (THIRD FROM LEFT), WITH THE HALFWAY HOUSE ORCHESTRA.

LOUIS ARMSTRONG, HOLDING TRUMPET, WITH THE HOT FIVE.

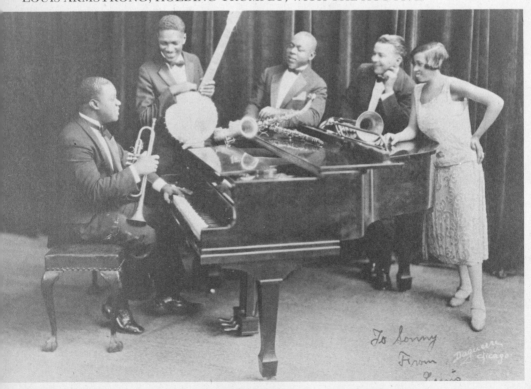

BIX BEIDERBECKE

EARL HINES,
WITH BUDD JOHNSON
ON SAXOPHONE.
Courtesy of RCA Victor Records.

FLETCHER HENDERSON (FOURTH FROM LEFT).

Photo by Duncan Scheidt.

CAB CALLOWAY

DUKE ELLINGTON

JACK TEAGARDEN

SIDNEY BECHET

FATS WALLER

DJANGO REINHARDT.
Photo by Jazz Hot.

ART TATUM

BENNY GOODMAN, WITH VOCALIST LOUISE TOBIN.

COUNT BASIE, WITH JO JONES ON DRUMS AND WALTER PAGE ON BASS.

BILLIE HOLIDAY.
Courtesy of Roy Hemming.

ROY ELDRIDGE, WITH
COUNT BASIE ON PIANO.

CHARLIE PARKER

NAT "KING" COLE.

Courtesy of Roy Hemming.

DIZZY GILLESPIE

THELONIOUS MONK

GERRY MULLIGAN

CLIFFORD BROWN.
Courtesy of Prestige Records.

CHET BAKER

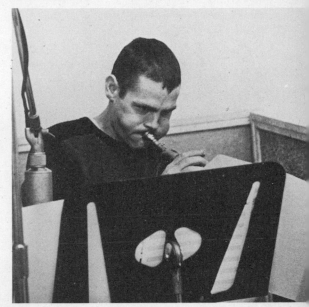

ELLA FITZGERALD

LAMBERT, HENDRICKS,
AND ROSS

BILL EVANS

JOHN COLTRANE

TANIA MARIA.
Courtesy of Concord Records.

WYNTON MARSALIS.
Photo by Mitchell Seidel.

ness of their improvisations left many scratching their heads. Jazz critics who'd enjoyed Basie, Goodman, and Ellington blasted the band for playing too cacophonously, while Kenton supporters—and there were thousands—insisted that this was the wave of the future, to which they felt the critics simply hadn't adapted yet.

Ironically, both were right. On the plus side, Kenton allowed his sidemen more creative freedom than any other bandleader before him, and many of them were truly great players. The rhythm section had a driving, pulsing feel that practically dragged the brass and reeds along with it, and— despite the complaints—the band turned out its quota of hit records. On the debit side, they did screech a lot more than other bands, providing little room for subtlety in their arrangements, and after the first few years, the Kenton style became as much of a "formula" as any other. At this point Kenton infused his band with strings and French horns, turning out more pop-styled arrangements and pretentious non-jazz music, such as Bob Graettinger's "City of Glass." This turned the band into truly a concert orchestra and divided the Kenton audience still further. The following album gives a pretty good idea of the Kenton style from 1943 to 1963:

> *The Jazz Compositions of Stan Kenton*/Eager Beaver; Opus in Pastels; Artistry Jumps; Lazey Dazey; Loco-Nova; Reflection; Theme for Sunday; Shelly Manne; Harlem Holiday; Concerto to End All Concertos; and Southern Scandal. Creative World ST-1078 (LP).

Now that the man himself—one of the most charming, aggressive, selfless, egotistical, stubborn, yet open-minded bundle of contradictions who ever lived—is gone, we can assess his legacy more objectively. And in light of the recordings, we can say that the critics were right: Kenton was a brilliant but erratic talent. In the album above, there is much to admire in the easy bounce of "Eager Beaver," the punchy swing in "Artistry Jumps," the rich sonorities of

"Opus in Pastels," "Lazey Dazey," and "Loco-Nova," and the exuberant, boppish sound of "Harlem Holiday." Conversely, his piano solo "Reflection" simply ruminates in a progressive stride style; "Shelly Manne" is stiffly pretentious; "Theme for Sunday" sounds like Mantovani or Percy Faith; and "Concerto to End All Concertos" is an infuriating blend of attractive, original ideas with tawdry sentimentality and easy solutions.

While opinion on the Kenton band was mixed, however, there were others that met with wider critical approval. Foremost among these was the group led by **Woody Herman** (1912–1988), former clarinetist and vocalist with Isham Jones's popular dance band, who suddenly began hiring the youngest, brightest white jazz talent around. Recruiter and cheerleader was bassist **Chubby Jackson** (1918–), who was like a divining rod for locating good new talent that Herman hadn't heard of.

Initially the assessment of drummer Dave Tough was anything but unanimous. One of the young Chicagoans who had played alongside Goodman, Frank Teschemacher, and Bud Freeman in the 1920s, and with the big bands of Goodman and Tommy Dorsey in the 1930s, Tough impressed Jackson as a shade too "old-fashioned" for the "new look." Herman stood by him, though, and eventually Jackson admitted he'd been wrong. Indeed, the rhythm section of Tough, Jackson, guitarist Billy Bauer, and pianist Ralph Burns turned out to be the finest in jazz since the "All-American Rhythm Section" of Basie, Green, Page, and Jones.

There were other stars in that band, soon nicknamed "The Herman Herd" or "The First Herd" (though Herman's previous band was also called The Herd): trumpeters Sonny Berman, Pete and Conte Candoli, Ray Wetzel, and Neal Hefti; trombonists Ed Kiefer and Bill Harris; saxists John La Porta, Flip Phillips, and Sam Marowitz; and a young woman vibist named Margie Hyams, who was replaced by the equally excellent Red Norvo. The arrangements by Hefti and Burns were wild, open, and imaginative; they spotlighted a bright trumpet/alto sax/clarinet-oriented sound without blatant blasting, unlike Kenton's style. For the second time, there was an all-white orchestra that could compete with Ellington consistently, on his own level.

Herman's group disbanded in December 1946 so he could be with his sick wife. But his retirement lasted just one year, and when he returned he took off in an entirely new direction. Whereas the previous Herd had been brash, daring, and "hot," the Second Herd was subtle, intricate, and "cool." Whereas the 1944–1946 band featured such firebrands as Candoli, Hefti, Phillips, La Porta, and Harris, the new one sported musicians such as Shorty Rogers, Ernie Royal, Stan Getz, Zoot Sims, and Earl Swope—all destined to lead the "cool school" of the 1950s. Burns returned as arranger, but now he was joined by Al Cohn, a young saxist/arranger with great promise.

The following editions of the Herman Herd, though often brilliant, have been offshoots of one of these two styles. Thus the following albums should be acquired by all who have an interest in changing styles:

> *The Thundering Herds*/Woodchopper's Ball; Apple Honey; Northwest Passage; Goosey Gander; The Good Earth; A Jug of Wine; Your Father's Moustache; Bijou; Wild Root; Panacea; Blues Are Brewing; Back Talk; Non-Alcoholic; The Goof and I; Four Brothers; and Blue Flame. CBS CJ/ CK-44108 (LP/CD).

> *The 1940s: The Small Groups*/Steps; Igor; Nero's Conception; Fan It; Pam; Someday, Sweetheart; I Surrender, Dear; Lost Weekend; Everywhere; Back Talk; With Someone New; and Wrap Your Troubles in Dreams (plus selections by Gene Krupa and Harry James). CBS CJ/CK/ CJT-44222 (LP/CD/Cs).

If bands such as Kenton's and Herman's were on the cutting edge of developing jazz trends, the orchestra led by bass saxist **Boyd Raeburn** (1913–1966) was essentially *sui* *generis.* It was originally a society band, a "mickey mouse" outfit that competed for jobs with Lawrence Welk; but Raeburn changed his mind about whether to follow his heart or his head when a horrible bus crash in late 1937 injured him severely and took the life of his friend bassist Homer Bennett. It took Raeburn roughly fourteen months to fulfill his contracted gigs and shed the strings and accordions, but by early 1939 he was fronting a fairly good swing outfit. Yet it was in Chicago, in 1943, that Raeburn put together what has been called the greatest jazz orchestra in history.

Pooling on whatever talent hadn't gone with the draft (Raeburn himself was 4-F), he decided he'd had enough, even with the compromises of the swing era. He played no "hits" unless they were songs he really liked, he avoided "popular" material unless his arrangers could transform it into pure jazz, the singers and players he hired were all first-rate musicians, and he made no money to speak of. Yet Boyd, who was himself a mediocre talent (he played bass sax, but only in ensembles), could get gigs and radio spots that were closed to others. Several of his musicians stayed with him despite the lack of cash, simply because they believed so much in what they were doing, while others outside the band gave Raeburn money to restart his orchestra every time it folded. In this helter-skelter, stop-start fashion, Boyd Raeburn managed to keep his magnificent organization together until 1948, when the money completely ran out.

Despite having different soloists over the years and several different arrangers contributing to the book, Raeburn's bands displayed a remarkable unity. Their sound was a mirror image of light bands such as Ellington's or the bright-sounding Herman Herd and was rooted in the low saxes (particularly baritone and bass), either by themselves or in mixtures with the brass. The voicings were highly unusual, using intervals that no contemporary musicians save Parker and Monk were into ("Tonsilectomy"), multitonal passages ("Dalvatore Sally"), and weird, offbeat figures ("March of the

Boyds") that no one else ever tried and that were excecuted with precision and élan. The arrangers who helped stretch the jazz vocabulary were Eddie Finckel, Budd Johnson, George Williams, Ralph Flanagan, Milt Kleeb, Dicky Wells, Dizzy Gillespie, and George Handy; the soloists included Gillespie, Eldridge, Berman, Benny Harris, Johnny Bothwell, Dodo Marmarosa, Tom Pederson, and Earl Swope, most of them before they gained fame with others' bands. In addition, the ensemble adopted a "legitimate" orchestral sound, which gave them a richness unlike any other. Just listening to the following recordings will convince any skeptic of this orchestra's superiority:

> *Boyd Raeburn: Rare Broadcast Performances*/Speak Low; Do Nothin' Til You Hear From Me; Street of Dreams; The Early Boyd; Night in Tunisia; I'll Remember April; Perdido; Sentimental Journey; Tush; Blue Moon; You've Got Me Crying Again; Sequence; I Cover the Waterfront; Laura; March of the Boyds; I Only Have Eyes for You; and Don't Take Your Love From Me. IAJRC (Stash) 48 (LP).

> *Boyd Raeburn*/Tonsilectomy; Forgetful; Rip Van Winkle; Yerxa; Memphis in June; I Don't Care Who Knows It; Boyd's Nest; Are You Livin', Old Man?; Blue Prelude; Picnic in the Wintertime; Boyd Meets Stravinsky; Where You At?; Out of This World; Personality; Dalvatore Sally; Blue Echoes; Two Spoos in an Igloo; Temptation; and Night in Tunisia. Echo Jazz EJCD-13 (CD, available from Stash).

Another pioneering band, albeit a less original one, was led at this same time by **Illinois Jacquet** (1921–), a tenor saxist who had come to prominence in the big bands of Lionel Hampton and Count Basie. Jacquet was unusual in that he was influenced by both Herschel Evans and Lester Young, and even a healthy dose of Ben Webster. As a result, Jacquet's style vacillated between hard-driving, riff-filled jazz, sometimes bordering on R&B, and straight-ahead bop based on the lessons of Young. The following album sums up his musical directions:

> *The Black Velvet Band*/Jet Propulsion; King Jacquet; Embryo; Riffin' at 24th Street; Mutton Leg; Symphony in Sid; A Jacquet for Jack the Bellboy; Big Foot; Black Velvet; B-Yot; Adam's Alley; Blue Satin; Slow Down, Baby; Hot Rod; You Gotta Change; and Flying Home. RCA Bluebird 6571-1/2/4-RB (LP/CD/Cs).

The above album is interesting for several reasons, not the least of which is the orchestration: In most of these cuts, Jacquet uses an eight-to-ten-piece band, a size that was to become standard in the late-bop and cool-jazz eras. Also of note is the prominence given to trombonist **J. J. Johnson** (1924–   ), the man who consolidated the staccato innovations of Dicky Wells with a wider range and greater imagination to make the trombone the equal of the trumpet and saxophone in bop. Sadly, one will notice that the later Jacquet recordings tend more toward R&B and away from bop. This was undoubtedly a commercial consideration, as both the Dizzy Gillespie and Erskine Hawkins big bands made similar concessions toward the end of their tenure with RCA Victor.

Even as Raeburn and Jacquet were recording their classic sides, however, an alternative direction was congealing in the styles of altoist **Charlie "Bird" Parker** (1920–1955) and trumpeter **John "Dizzy" Gillespie** (1917–   ), with more than a little assistance from pianist/composer/arranger **Thelonious Monk** (1920–1982).

Parker, an alumnus of the Kansas City-styled big band of Jay McShann, had been "fooling around" with upper harmonics—ninths, elevenths, and thirteenths—since about 1939. In the early 1940s, at a Harlem Club called Minton's Playhouse, Gillespie and Monk were also looking for something. When they all came together in 1944 and 1945, bebop was born.

Put as simply as possible, bebop was swing music turned

inside out. If a swing drummer played beats one and three, the bop drummer would emphasize two and four—or any beats that took his fancy, if that's what he felt like. Since swing drummers laid heavy emphasis on the bass drum and tom-toms, the bop drummer played mostly high up, on the snares and cymbals. Because swing bands usually played reeds versus brass, the bop bands (such as Raeburn's) mixed sections. Solos tended to be more frantic, with plenty of six-teenth and thirty-second notes, exploring variations on the harmony rather than the melody. At such high speeds they also altered the concept of rhythm, moving away from un-even ("swinging") pairs of notes to even ("bopping") figures. And last, the boppers tried to reject or at least alter the regular Tin Pan Alley tunes that swing musicians played. Their compositions, though based on changes of some early songs, had more unusual chording, often in rising or de-scending chromatics, and melodies that were in themselves authentic jazz compositions (for instance, Dizzy Gillespie's "Groovin' High" as an improvisation on the chord pattern of "Whispering"). Like critic Stanley Dance, I am not alto-gether convinced that bop was a better or more creative way of playing jazz it was simply different, more harmonically advanced, and inevitably more difficult to do well. This is one reason why the great interpreters of bop during the period from 1945 to 1955 amount to less than two dozen, whereas there were scores of excellent jazz musicians working in older idioms.

There is, luckily, a record showing the fascinating devel-opment of this music at its roots: a transcript made at Min-ton's Playhouse in May 1941. Though some swing elements are naturally still prevalent and two "standards" are used, their treatment is already moving in different directions. The band members are noteworthy; trumpeters Gillespie and Joe Guy, tenor saxist Don Byas, baritonist Nick Fenton, guitarist Charlie Christian, pianists Thelonious Monk and Ken Ker-sey, and drummer Kenny Clarke. The presence of Christian is significant, showing a general tendency toward players who were strong soloists instead of "rhythm men" who faded into the background, such as Fred Guy or Freddie Green. Truly, Django Reinhardt's influence was never more strongly felt:

Charlie Christian with Dizzy Gillespie & Thelonious Monk/ Stompin' at the Savoy; Stardust; Up on Teddy's Hill; Kerouac; and Guy's Got to Go. Up Front UPF-181 (OP).

In 1945 a small label called Musicraft (and its offshoot, Guild) became the first to record and issue the "new music" commercially. Gillespie's quintet made "Groovin' High," included on *Jazz Vol. 11*, and others that first confused and then influenced many others. The first Gillespie group wasn't all bop, though including Parker and Clarke; with guitarist Tiny Grimes and bassist Slam Stewart still playing swing, the band had a somewhat mixed style. Nevertheless, the 1945 Musicrafts are the first bop records.

After this initial stage of togetherness, however, the bop pioneers went essentially different ways. Gillespie formed the first bop big band, one that enjoyed unusual popular success for so experimental a group (possibly due to a general public interest in "new" things, as well as the pioneering of Kenton). Despite the fact that Monk was an arranger for a time, both he and Parker tended to prefer the intimacy of small groups. Strangely, they even chose separate paths, crossing only momentarily in the years to come.

As Parker exerted more and more influence on the upcoming jazz generation, there came an inherent danger. In such a high-speed, high-tech sort of music, many younger players could only assimilate the exterior shell; like young Roy Eldridge, they could play fast but nothing of quality. Parker was the total antithesis of this. He seldom if ever played anything that was not so logically constructed it couldn't be taken apart and put back together like clockwork, even though it was all spontaneously improvised. He is the second great legend in jazz, often viewed as a tragic figure, though he actually created most of his own problems (primarily drug addiction and a seriously antisocial personality). Unlike Beiderbecke, however, he at least lived to see his influence take root in others.

Parker's alto had a beautiful, full tone with a strange, unmistakable rasp. This, as the birth pains he experienced in producing his memorable and remarkable solos, made his playing unique. It's impossible to confuse Parker with any other sax player who ever lived, and that—in addition to his creativity—would be enough to place him in the very highest ranks. His solos were so alive, so bursting with ideas that each chorus could in itself have been spread over three minutes by other players. Since his style changed little once he'd found the way, it is difficult to say whether he would have evolved farther had he lived—but that's academic. The truth is, Parker's playing *was* the truth. He never clowned, never played the fool or cheated. Every time he went out on the stand, a part of himself was exposed for all to hear. The records he made for Savoy between 1945 and 1948, and the sides for Dial in 1946 and 1947, are considered his finest and are conveniently collected in two albums:

The Savoy Recordings: Master Takes/Tiny's Tempo; Red Cross; Ko-Ko; Warming Up on a Riff; Billie's Bounce; Now's the Time; Chasin' the Bird; Thriving on a Riff; Donna Lee; Cheryl; Little Willie Leaps; Milestone; Half Nelson; Another Hair-Do; Bluebird; Bird Gets the Worm; Klaunstance; Ah-Leu-Cha; Barbados; Perhaps; Constellation; Parker's Mood; Marmaduke; Steeple Chase; and Merry-Go-Round. Savoy Jazz SJL-2201/ZD-70737 (two LPs/one CD).

The Legendary Dial Masters, Vol. 1/Diggin' Diz; Yardbird Suite; Moose the Mooche; Ornithology; Night in Tunisia; Lover Man; Max Making Wax; The Gypsy; Bebop; This Is Always; Dark Shadows; The Hymn; Bird's Nest; Cool Blues; Relaxin' at Camarillo; Bird Feathers; Cheers; Carvin' the Bird; Stupendous; Dexterity; Bird of Paradise; Bongo Bop; Dewey Square; Klact-Oveeseds-Tene; and Embraceable You. Stash ST-CD-23 (CD).

While Parker was making history with Savoy and Dial, Gillespie was doing it with RCA Victor and—later—his own label, Dee Gee. In their day, Gillespie's big-band sides were criticized for their tubby, dry sound, but while the technical aspects of the recordings could have been better, the playing coud scarcely be so:

> *Dizziest*/52nd Street Theme; Night in Tunisia; Ol' Man Rebop; Anthropology; Ow!; Oop-Pop-a-Da; Two Bass Hit; Stay on It; Algo Bueno; Cool Breeze; Cubana Be, Cubana Bop; Manteca; Good Bait; Woody'n You; Ool-Ya-Koo; Minor Walk; Guarachi Guaro; Lover Come Back to Me; Duff Capers, Swedish Suite; St. Louis Blues; I Should Care; That Old Black Magic; You Go to My Head; Dizzier and Dizzier; Jump Did-Le Ba; Hey Pete! Let's Eat Mo' Meat; I'm Beboppin' Too; In the Land of Oo-Bla-Dee; If Love Is Trouble; and Jumpin' With Symphony Sid. RCA Bluebird 5785-1/4-RB (two LPs/one Cs).

Just for the record, the first four cuts are by his septet. Monk wrote the first, Gillespie the second, Leonard Feather the third, and Parker the fourth. "Cubana Be, Cubana Bop," composed by George Russell, contains a modal introduction that was ten years ahead of its time and the fiery conga drums of **Chano Pozo Gonzales** (1918–1948), who died shortly thereafter. Pozo's influence on Latin jazz, especially the percussion, is still felt. Gillespie's band used more riffs than did other boppers. Though he accented off-rhythms and utilized a lot of percussion, most of his best-known records ("Manteca," "Ow!," "Stay on It," "Cool Breeze," and "Cubana Be") are quite riff-filled. But the music they played was pure bebop: the high cymbal work, the saxes playing convoluted sixteenth notes, and the trumpets sounded like five Dizzys.

Before long, Gillespie had his followers in the "new style," both black and white musicians. Among the former was **Theodore "Fats" Navarro** (1924–1950), one of the more interesting players in the bop movement. The new Fats was a trumpeter of both dazzling speed and tremendous warmth, exhibiting a round tone and depth that were unusual in one so young. In addition, he seemed to grasp the inherent difficulties of bop almost instinctively, was able to fit into any context, and usually played to his utmost. As a result, he was an invaluable session man in the late 1940s, particularly on those dates when a "substitute Dizzy" was called for. On some of the following cuts he is teamed with several musicians who were associated with Gillespie, including altoist Ernie Henry, vibist Milt Jackson, drummer Kenny Clarke, bongo player Chano Pozo Gonzales, and vocalist Kenny Hagood. Also present are such important transitional figures as trumpeter Howard McGhee (who also became a sort of "surrogate Dizzy" for several of Parker's sessions), plus tenor saxists Allen Eager and **Wardell Gray** (1921–1955), the latter of whom became a semilegend himself (he can also be heard on Parker's "Relaxin' at Camarillo" session):

> *The Fabulous Fats Navarro, Vol. 2* (OP)/The Skunk; Double Talk; Lady Bird; Jahbero; Symphonette (two tks. each; Boperation; and I Think I'll Go Away. Blue Note B11E/CDP/B41E-81532-2 (LP/CD/Cs).

In 1949 Gray was a member of the short-lived Benny Goodman bop band, but he became far more famous from a recording he made for Dial Records, with fellow tenor player **Dexter Gordon** (1927–1990), called "The Chase." In 1952, during a Gene Norman "Just Jazz" concert in Pasadena, they rejoined forces to encore that underground "hit" as well as to add a further example of extended chase-chorus playing in Charlie Parker's "The Steeple Chase." Their contrasting styles were interesting: Gordon with a heavy, thick tone, somewhere between Hawkins and Sonny Rollins, playing musical ideas heavily borrowed from Illinois Jacquet; and Gray, fleet, lithe, somewhat in the Lester Young tradition but with a more beautiful tone and sharper "bite." The results can be heard on *The Chase and The Steeple Chase* (MCA/MCAC-

1336, LP/Cs), along with recordings by Kansas City tenorman Paul Quinichette.

One of the few white musicians to play in the Gillespie style was **Conte Candoli**, fresh from the Woody Herman First Herd, where he had begun as a follower of Eldridge. Candoli lacked Navarro's warmth but made up for it with a perfect embouchure and a secure high range that allowed him flights of fancy almost as spectacular as those of Charlie Shavers. Candoli played in the late 1940s with the bop septet of tenor saxist **Charlie Ventura** (1916–1992), a player whose tone and style seemed more in line with the "booting" post-swing style of Georgia Auld than the new "cool" sound. Nevertheless, Ventura's group could generate some very vital excitement, especially with such sidemen as Candoli, trombonist Benny Green, Parker disciple Boots Mussilli, drummer Ed Shaughnessy, and two early but interesting bop scatters, Jackie Cain and Roy Kral (known professionally simply as Jackie and Roy):

> *A Charlie Ventura Concert*/Yesterdays; The Peanut Vendor; Euphoria; Fine and Dandy; East of Suez; If I Had You; I'm Forever Blowing Bubbles; Pennies from Heaven; and How High the Moon. MCA/MCAD/MCAC-42330 (LP/CD/Cs).

While Parker, Gillespie, Navarro, and Ventura were garnering the plaudits of jazz fans, however, Thelonious Monk was sitting quietly in the background—that is, until October 1947, when Alfred Lion of Blue Note Records convinced him to start recording. If Gillespie was the head of the bop revolution and Parker its heart, Monk was surely its soul. Never a flashy pianist, he was not even really a bopper at heart. The slowness of his technique excluded him from the fast company of Tatum, Cole, and Bud Powell, who was the true inventor of bop piano. Monk preferred writing his own material rather than merely adapting previously existing chord patterns. Weird harmonies were commonplace in his music, as were unresolved chords, so that Mary Lou Williams called it "Chinese music." But Monk created hardly that. More accurately, as Ralph Berton has pointed out, Monk was the Stravinsky of jazz. Like Stravinsky, he used stiff, formal rhythms to offset more fluid ones, a practice that not even Gillespie or Parker could emulate. Monk made the first successful experiments in tempos other than 4/4, and even within that time-honored tempo his compositions bore little resemblance to standards. Uncertain tonality became a Monk trademark, one he bore proudly. So did "layered tempos," where he would offset a basic 4/4 with figures in 3/4, 5/4, even 6/8. It took a lot of guts to play some of his more complex compositions and still improvise on them, and he was aware of that, too. Thus for years the only versions we had of most of them were his own:

> *Thelonious Monk: The Complete Genius/*'Round Midnight; In Walked Bud; Monk's Mood; Who Knows; Off Minor; Thelonious; Humph; Suburban Eyes; Evonce; Ruby My Dear; April in Paris; Nice Work If You Can Get It; Well, You Needn't; I Mean You; Introspection; I Should Care; Evidence; Epistrophy; All the Things You Are; Mysterioso (two tks.); Let's Cool One; Carolina Moon; Mornin' In; Ask Me Now; Skippy; Straight, No Chaser; Four in One (two tks.); Criss Cross; Willow, Weep for Me; and Eronel. Blue Note LWB-00579/CDP-81510/11 (two LPs/CDs—CDs omit July 1948 session with Milt Jackson).

It is interesting to note that on these records the sidemen are those who would come to prominence in the next decade: trumpeters Kenny Dorham and Idrees Sulieman, alto saxists Sahib Shihab and Lou Donaldson, and drummer **Art Blakey** (1919–1990). Monk had to be careful in selecting musicians who could be comfortable in his idiom; small wonder he had to find those who weren't in the mainstream. There is a great deal to be said about most of these sides, but suffice it to mention that " 'Round Midnight" was his unofficial theme song; "Epistrophy" is a successful splice of 4/4 and 6/8 rhythm; "In Walked Bud," "Skippy," and "Straight, No Chaser" are superb examples of his art; and "Carolina Moon" is a famous transformation of a pop standard into a 6/8 jazz waltz.

Blakey, in fact, was so enamored of the Monk concept that he built an entire career around it. This began in the early 1950s with the original Jazz Messengers, a small band co-led by Blakey and pianist Horace Silver. Even after Silver left to form his own groups, Blakey continued, unabated, in the same vein for the next four decades. Over the years, his Jazz Messengers have been as famous for their "graduates" as for the swinging, hard-bop music they played. Among these have been alto saxist Jackie McLean, tenorman Johnny Griffin, and a string of trumpeters including Clifford Brown, Donald Byrd, Bill Hardman, Lee Morgan, Freddie Hubbard, and Wynton Marsalis. Though the following album was recorded in 1956–1957, it strongly represents the postwar musical concepts of the Monk ensembles, with unified compositions in which the soloists contribute to the whole:

> *Art Blakey: The Jazz Messenger*/Ecaroh; Cranky Spanky; Stella by Starlight; Hank's Symphony; Little Melonae; Infra-Rae; Carol's Interlude; and The New Message. CBS CK/CT-47119 (CD/Cs).

The other pianist who most greatly influenced his peers was **Bud Powell** (1924–1966), a tortured soul who, like Bolden and Rappolo, suffered from mental illness. Unlike them, he managed to return temporarily to sanity a few times. Bouncing from pillar to post, from mental breakdown to concert hall, Powell was in and out of music throughout the last decade of his life. Earlier, however, he had it all together. Strongly influenced by Tatum and Nat Cole, Powell changed the function of the pianist in both bands and small groups from that of chordist and occasional soloist to someone who was continually involved in the ongoing process of harmonic substitution and melodic improvisation.

The following album, though recorded late in his career, shows how he adapted the Nat Cole style of piano to his own means, generally dispensing altogether with the left hand except as occasional punctuation, and developing the right to cascades of Tatum-like brilliance without having to utilize the pearly arpeggios that sometimes marred Tatum's playing. The first six selections are rather nervous-sounding, but the remainder represent the Powell style at its most riveting:

> *Time Was*/There Will Never Be Another You; They Didn't Believe Me; I Cover the Waterfront; Time Was; Topsy Turvy; Elegy; Coscrane; Jump City; Blues for Bessie; Salt Peanuts; Swedish Pastry; Shaw Nuff; Midway; Oblivion; Get It; Another Dozen; She; and Birdland Blues. RCA 63687-2-RB (CD).

In 1953, at Massey Hall in Toronto, Canada, the giants of bop—Parker, Gillespie, Powell, Max Roach, and bassist Charlie Mingus—came together for a single concert of such brilliance that it has remained an indelible tribute to their musical battles:

> *The Quintet*/Perdido; Salt Peanuts; All the Things You Are; Wee; Hot House; and A Night in Tunisia. Debut OJC/ OJCCD-044-2 (LP/CD).

Though bop continued to be played for several more years, this concert represents both a sort of apotheosis and Götterdämmerung of the style. Within three years Parker was dead, Mingus was heading in new directions, and Powell was institutionalized again. Yet these five pioneers produced that night a lasting memorial to the music they'd fought for, and their playing was a stunning vindication.

The new trend coming up was being spearheaded on the East Coast by trumpeter Miles Davis and on the West Coast by baritone saxist Gerry Mulligan. Eventually the bulk of the new sound was concentrated on the West Coast, but not before it was given a name—and that name was "cool."

6.
The Birth of the Cool

Though sometimes forgotten, the first real example of cool jazz on records was the 1940s orchestra of pianist **Claude Thornhill** (1906–1965). A classically trained pianist, Thornhill combined the harmonies of Debussy with the harmonies of Charlie Parker, created an ethereal sound in which the rhythm section subtly propelled the beat, and emphasized the use of woodwinds and French horns. He combined compositions of Tchaikovsky with those of Illinois Jacquet, added airy solos by altoist **Lee Konitz** (1927–), and added even airier arrangements by **Gil Evans** (1912–1988) to create the first big band to focus on introspection rather than a large, brassy sound. Indeed, Thelonious Monk paid them the ultimate compliment, calling Thornhill's "the only really good big band I've heard in years." As the following album shows, this was scarcely exaggeration on Monk's part:

Best of the Big Bands: Claude Thornhill/Snowfall; A Sunday Kind of Love; Arab Dance; Where or When; Robbin's Nest; Early Autumn; Hungarian Dance #5; There's a Small Hotel; Portrait of a Guinea Farm; Yardbird Suite; I Knew You When; Anthropology; Stealin' Apples; Under the Willow Tree; Buster's Last Stand; and Let's Call It a Day. CBS CK/CT-46152 (CD/Cs).

Naturally, the commercial side of the Thornhill band is represented here, primarily in the dated vocals by Buddy Hughes, Fran Warren, and a group called The Snowflakes, but even in such arrangements Thornhill stayed true to the transparent sound that was his trademark. Even more astonishing, however, is his permutation of Fats Waller's "Stealin' Apples" from a Henderson-*cum*-Goodman swing vehicle to a personal statement by his band, as well as the mind-boggling complexity of the 1941 "Portrait of a Guinea Farm"—both made *before* Evans or the French horns came into the picture. Despite Thornhill's accomplishments, however, the real breakthrough into the "cool era" came a few years later, in 1949.

Originally they started out in the same place at the same time, with the same idea: **Miles Davis** (1926–1991) and **Gerry Mulligan** (1927–), pioneers of the new sound. Not that they were alone by any means. Konitz and Gil Evans were there, along with pianist **Al Haig** (1923–1982), French hornist and arranger **Gunther Schuller** (1925–), and drummers Kenny Clarke and Max Roach. What they saw, led by a few Thornhill records, was a vision of music as an opaque, impressionist drawing in which all is vague and nothing definite. Their music still had a beat, but the textures used were in soft, warm colors rather than hard, brilliant ones. They (again) brought the tuba back into jazz, this time as a low horn instead of a beatkeeper; they introduced the French horn for texture; and they used cornets and flugelhorns as often as the more piercing trumpet.

Davis's Birth of the Cool tuba band made its debut in 1949. It played two dates at Birdland, recorded twelve sides for Capitol, and then disbanded. Their recorded legacy, however, was so strong an influence that several groups sprang up trying to emulate their sound:

The Complete Birth of the Cool/Jeru; Move; Godchild; Budo; Moon Dreams; Venus de Milo; Rogue; Boplicity; Israel;

Rocker; Deception; and Darn That Dream. Capitol N-16168/CDP-92862 (LP/CD).

Pianist John Lewis arranged "Budo," "Rogue," and "Move"; "Deception" was written and arranged by Davis; and "Boplicity" and "Moon Dreams" were arranged by Evans. The others were arranged by Mulligan, including three original compositions. One of these, "Jeru," alternates between 3/4 and 4/4 time, showing some Monk influence. In later years, Mulligan used these sounds and textures as the bases for his own nonet, tentette, and big band.

When Mulligan returned to the West Coast, he formed a combo with drummer Chico Hamilton, bassist Bobby Whitlock, and trumpeter **Chet Baker** (1929–1988), a lyrical player in the Beiderbecke-Davis mold. Baker became a genuine matinee idol in the 1950s; his baby face, soft and sweet singing, and James Dean-like clothing led many to overlook his playing, which was exceptionally beautiful and original. Baker and Mulligan parted company in 1957, and Baker's life unfortunately degenerated into heroin addiction. However, their 1952–53 recordings remain classics:

The Best of the Gerry Mulligan Quartet with Chet Baker/Bernie's Tune; Nights at the Turntable; Freeway; Soft Shoe; Walkin' Shoes; Makin' Whoopee; Carson City Stage; My Old Flame; Love Me or Leave Me; Swinghouse; Jeru; Darn That Dream; I'm Beginning to See the Light; My Funny Valentine; and Festive Minor. Pacific Jazz CDP7-95481 (CD).

As can be garnered from this album, their playing had an almost baroque quality, in which both rhythmic and harmonic alterations crossed each other with dazzling speed, even in such ballads as "My Funny Valentine." There were never any "gaps" in their duo performances, since each was adept at anticipating the other's changes. As a result, the continuity of their music became its most expressive quality, offsetting the "cool" sound of their instruments. The heat of the music was cerebral and subtle, though each of them could at times play unexpected bursts that made the baroque quality all the more fascinating.

Even though few players came close to the special camaraderie they had, the Mulligan-Baker interplay and the orchestration of the Davis-Mulligan nonet inspired dozens of combos throughout the 1950s. Among the best of these was **Shorty Rogers** (1925–) and his Giants, a small band that contained refugees from the Woody Herman and Stan Kenton bands: alto saxist Art Pepper, tenor saxist Jimmy Giuffre, French hornist John Graas, and drummer Shelly Manne. Like the Davis band, the Giants had a hard-driving, swinging rhythmic core that propelled the music well and, like the Mulligan-Baker Quartet, had the distinction of being an all-*jazz* outfit. Its only drawback was a tendency toward sameness in the arrangements, though in its heyday (roughly from 1952 to 1958) it was an extremely influential band. And, as the following album demonstrates, its music still sounds fresh:

> *Short Stops*/Powder Puff; The Pesky Serpent; Bunny; Pirouette; Morpo; Diablo's Dance; Mambo del Crow; Indian Club; Coop de Graas; Infinity Promenade; Short Stop; Boar-Jibu; Contours; Tale of an African Lobster; Chiquito Loco; Sweetheart of Sigmund Freud; Blues for Brando; Chino; The Wild One (Hot Blood); and Windswept. RCA Bluebird 5917-1/2/4-RB (two LPs/one CD/two Cs).

Another superb yet vastly underrated player of the cool-bop school was clarinetist **Boniface "Buddy" De Franco** (1923–), a player who for many years was a virtuoso improviser who "got no respect." Despite having an even finer tone and technique than Artie Shaw, De Franco soon discovered that there was no place for the clarinet in the postwar world of honking tenors and bebop alto saxes. He briefly led his own big band, 1948–1949, which recorded a handful of sides for Capitol (but were unissued until the 1970s!), but

which came to the fore during the early 1950s as the result
of a series of superb small-group recordings for Verve. European critics were occasionally severe toward De Franco,
constantly labeling his style as not merely cool, but cold. In
relistening to him today, however, one realizes that this was
simply because his technique, including his tone production,
was so classical—which it had to be to play bop. The following
album, made in 1956, illustrates his abilities to match musical
wits with one of the greatest geniuses in jazz:

> *Art Tatum–Buddy De Franco*/Deep Night; This Can't Be
> Love; Memories of You; Once in a While; A Foggy Day;
> Lover Man; You're Mine You; and Makin' Whoopee.
> Pablo 2310/52310-736, 2405-430-2 (LP/Cs/CD).

In this album, one can appreciate the richness of De Franco's tone as well as an even rarer sense of Romanticism in
his performance of "Deep Night," while on the up-tempo
tunes he becomes the only soloist in the Group Masterpieces
series to give Tatum a run for his money. Tatum, challenged
here as in no other recording, responds with some of his
most impressive single-note playing, leaving no doubt that
he was the principal inspirator of Bud Powell. Sadly, this was
the apex of De Franco's career; despite his brilliance, he was
later reduced to leading the Glenn Miller "ghost band" in an
effort to make enough money to compensate for his extraordinary talent. In recent years he has reemerged, as brilliant
and perfect as ever, and just as neglected by the critical jazz
fraternity.

Ultimately the emergence of West Coast cool led to a rift.
It became associated with young, white Californians, while
"tougher" East Coast blacks continued to play bop. Obviously
a catalyst was needed to make the new cool acceptable to the
majority of jazz musicians, while still retaining enough bop
qualities to placate those who'd gotten used to the Parker-
Gillespie style. Since both bop and cool, as we've seen, were
the products of collaborative minds rather than individuals,

a unique musical genius was clearly needed. In 1953 that genius was found and recorded; sadly, he hadn't long to live and develop.

This was trumpeter **Clifford Brown** (1930–1956), the third great legend in jazz. Unlike Beiderbecke and Parker, however, his legendary status is not based on a lack of recognition or a tortured life, but because his talent was greater than that of any contemporary soloist. The mere fact that he played in roughly the same historical period as Parker needn't deter us from accepting him as a true great. Even Parker and Gillespie were literally flabbergasted by the musical maturity of this young man. Like Art Tatum, Clifford Brown neatly and effortlessly summed up everything that had gone before him in the history of his instrument. He had the fat, rich tone of a Beiderbecke, the *joie de vivre* of an Armstrong, the excitement and drive of an Eldridge, the harmonic daring and speed of a Gillespie, and a very personal warmth all his own. His breath control was stupendous; sometimes Brown could play an entire half chorus without taking a breath. His embouchure was absolutely perfect, allowing him complete virtuosic control, yet he never showed off for the sake of mere flash, as Eldridge and Gillespie did in their early days. Brown had a brilliant mathematical mind that enabled him to balance his phrases in a way that has hardly been duplicated since. In short, he was a very serious musician, with a firm idea of expanding the vocabulary of his instrument.

He began by gigging around his hometown, Wilmington, Delaware, and in nearby Philadelphia. He was seriously injured in a car crash in 1950, a portent of things to come, and remained immobile and inactive for nearly a year. Following that, he played with a rhythm-and-blues group, Chris Powell and his Blue Flames, for about a year and made his first recordings with them in early 1952. Then he left and began playing around New York for a while. His first jazz records were cut as part of saxist Lou Donaldson's quintet, in June 1953. After a few more dates, Brown joined Tadd Dameron's

Discovering Great Jazz

band for the summer in Atlantic City, then became a member of Lionel Hampton's all-star orchestra for a tour of Scandinavia and France.

. While in Europe, Brown made a number of discs with Lionel Hampton's big band and various small groups. When he returned, he played briefly in Art Blakey's Jazz Messengers and then went to California at the request of drummer Max Roach. The two formed a partnership that would last until Brown's death, in another car crash, in late June 1956.

Brown made so many recordings, all of outstanding quality, that one hardly knows where to begin, but the following three albums display his versatility, influence, and maturity over three years:

> *Clifford Brown Memorial*/Philly J.J.; Dial B for Beauty; Choose Now; Theme of No Repeat; Stockholm Sweetnin'; Falling in Love with Love; 'Scuse These Blues; and Lover Come Back to Me. Prestige OJC/OJCCD-017 (LP/CD).

> *Clifford Brown & Max Roach*/Delilah; Parisian Thoroughfare; The Blues Walk; Daahoud; Joy Spring; Jordu; and What Am I Here For? EmArcy EXPR-1033/814 645-2 (LP/CD).

> *At Basin Street*/What Is This Thing Called Love?; Love Is a Many-Splendored Thing; I'll Remember April; Powell's Prances; Time; The Scene Is Clean; and Gertrude's Bounce. EmArcy EXPR-1031/814 648-2 (LP/CD).

The first album displays his impact on the hard-bop band of Dameron and the cool octet of baritone saxist Lars Gullin, a Swedish disciple of Mulligan's. The second features the famous Brown-Roach Quintet with tenor saxist Harold Land, pianist Richie Powell (Bud Powell's younger brother), and bassist George Morrow, as well as three classics written by Brown: "Daahoud," "The Blues Walk," and "Joy Spring."

Harold Land was a player in the hard-bop mold, but in late 1955 he was replaced by an important transitional figure, **Sonny Rollins** (1929–). Rollins's concept of the tenor sax was as different from Lester Young as Young had been from Hawkins. Instead of a fat, rich tone or an airy, breathy one, Rollins purveyed a flat, tubular quality, something not far removed from the sound of a car horn. One should not misconstrue this as negative criticism, but merely an attempt to describe what's difficult to put into words.

Artistically, Rollins was a superb craftsman who improvised in angular lines rather than a smooth curve. This, too, was a radical departure, even from boppers such as Wardell Gray and Dexter Gordon or cool players such as Stan Getz. In short, the Rollins sound was not to everyone's liking, but he was gutsy and brilliant and helped shape the wave of the future just as strongly as Brown. The modern sound of the tenor saxophone dates directly from Rollins's first recordings, which are heard in the third of these albums.

After two albums with the Roach-Brown Quintet—one under Brown's name and one for Prestige under his own— Rollins cut his own landmark album, *Saxophone Colossus*. This in turn led to the remarkable "Freedom Suite," which extended extemporaneous sax playing in a way unparalleled at the time, as well as to recordings with such major jazz figures as Thelonious Monk. The following album gives a panoramic perspective on this most fruitful period in Rollins's career, one that jazz buffs look back on as his coming out:

> *The Essential Sonny Rollins*/Pannonica; La Villa; Ev'ry Time We Say Goodbye; Dearly Beloved; Cutie; The Last Time I Saw Paris; Happiness Is Just a Thing Called Joe; The Freedom Suite; and Someday I'll Find You. Riverside FCD-60-020 (CD).

After the "crossover" success of Brown and Rollins, doors opened in the East to other West Coast musicians. One of the best of the white players was alto saxist **Art Pepper** (1925–1982). Following a stint with Stan Kenton's big band in the 1940s, Pepper garnered much acclaim in the 1950s for playing in a cross between the hard-bop of Parker and Mussilli and the soft-cool of Konitz and Paul Desmond. In the late 1950s, his acceptance in the coterie of East Coast hard boppers became complete when he recorded a now classic album with Miles Davis's rhythm section of pianist Red Garland, bassist Paul Chambers, and drummer Philly Joe Jones. It combined originals, pop standards, bop standards, and even one Dixieland number:

> *Art Pepper Meets the Rhythm Section*/You'd Be So Nice to Come Home To; Red Pepper Blues; Imagination; Waltz Me Blues; Straight Life; Jazz Me Blues; Tin Tin Deo; Star Eyes; and Birks Works. Contemporary OJC/OJCCD-338-2 (LP/CD).

Pepper's treatment of these numbers bears some consideration in detail, particularly in "Star Eyes," where his playing is anything but the considered calm of Miles Davis's solo with Charlie Parker, and "Jazz Me Blues," where Pepper is obviously enjoying himself while transforming the Dixieland-Chicago rhythm into something very modern and completely free of cliché. He might well have gone on to become a real force in the evolution of jazz in the 1960s, but his drug habit interfered. Not until the late 1970s was he able to play with the command he exhibits here, and with even greater insight.

All of the foregoing represent changes and evolutions within the jazz community. Yet insofar as the public was concerned, much of the new jazz was too confusing, too much unlike the sounds they had grown up with during the swing era to communicate anything to them. As a result, there grew out of the mélange of the jazz mainstream two players whose playing was simple enough to capture the imagination of the layman without compromising their standards as creative musicians.

The first of these, pianist **Erroll Garner** (1923–1977), provided a simplified version of the Tatum style. As a somewhat limited technician (like Monk), Garner played dragged, single-note lines in the right hand while the left strummed arpeggios in a guitarlike fashion; Tatum's out-of-tempo introductions were reduced, in Garner, to abstract opening cadenzas. Unlike Tatum, however, who took his playing very, very seriously, Garner displayed an odd, pixieish sense of humor that also did not fail to appeal to the masses. He began recording in the 1940s, first with the Slam Stewart Trio and then in a memorable (if oddly mixed) session with Charlie Parker. But it was with the Mercury label in the 1950s that he made his first great breakthrough, and this was the album (and title cut) that did it:

> *The Original Misty*/Misty; Rosalie; I've Got the World on a String; 7-11 Jump; Don't Worry 'Bout Me; You Are My Sunshine; Part Time Blues; All of a Sudden; In a Mellow Tone; There's a Small Hotel; I Wanna Be a Rug Cutter; Exactly Like You; and Oh, Lady Be Good. Mercury 834910-2/4 (CD/Cs).

There is a terrible irony and sadness in the fact that "Misty" became the piano-lounge song *sine qua non*. Hearing the freshness of Garner's conception as he *improvised* it into being on that long-ago day in 1954, one is struck by the Bix Beiderbecke-like intensity of his lyricism. One could with justice imagine that, had Bix lived longer and switched to piano permanently, he might very well have become Erroll Garner. This is borne out in the intense swing yet quirky improvisations featured in "7-11 Jump," "I Wanna Be a Rug Cutter," and "Exactly Like You," which show the side of Garner's art that no one dared copy because no one (save Bobby Enriquez) could.

The other great popular favorite of the 1950s (and early 1960s) was former Woody Herman tenorman **Stan Getz** (1927–1991). One of the greatest improvisers in jazz, Getz stubbornly clung to a romantic expression in defiance of his era—as well as in defense of his "cool" tone, very much a descendant of Lester Young's. His tours with Norman Granz's Jazz at the Philharmonic in 1957 brought out a more emotional side of Getz, as well as a slightly more daring improviser. He became even better known in the early-to-mid-1960s as the progenitor of the bossa nova style, a highly artificial, somewhat limited hybrid of classical and Latin elements. But his greatest achievement as a jazz musician was summed up in an album he made during that breakthrough year of 1957 with three like-minded pros: pianist **Oscar Peterson** (1925–), who emulated the technical speed of Art Tatum without exploring the lightning-quick harmonic substitutions; guitarist Herb Ellis, a devoted disciple of Charlie Christian; and bassist Ray Brown, one of the few great powerhouse bassists of the 1950s. The ensuing collection became an instant classic, and it remains so to this day:

> *Stan Getz & the Oscar Peterson Trio*/I Want to Be Happy; Pennies From Heaven; Bewitched, Bothered, and Bewildered; I Don't Know Why; How Long Has This Been Going On; I Can't Get Started; Polka Dots and Moonbeams; I'm Glad There Is You; Tour's End; I Was Doing All Right; Bronx Blues; Three Little Words; Detour Ahead; Sunday; and Blues for Henry. Verve 827826-2/4 (CD/Cs).

Indeed, as if to answer the charge that bop and cool were somehow "superior" to the old swing style, one of jazz's old-timers—all but forgotten by younger jazz fans—revived his career during this period to produce music of lasting value. This was **Henry "Red" Allen** (1908–1967), veteran of the King Oliver, Jelly Roll Morton, and Louis Armstrong bands (among others), who had matured into one of the great individualists in jazz. In the company of such swing-era stalwarts as Coleman Hawkins, Buster Bailey, J. C. Higginbotham, and Cozy Cole, Allen's trumpet playing on his 1957 Victor album (recently reissued) presented his finest testament on records:

> *World On a String*/Love Is Just Around the Corner; Let Me Miss You, Baby; Ride, Red, Ride; I Cover the Water-

front; 'Swonderful; St. James Infirmary; Algiers Bounce; Love Me or Leave Me; I've Got the World on a String; Ain't She Sweet; and Sweet Lorraine. RCA Bluebird 2497-2-RB (CD).

In addition to his usual asymmetrical phrase-shapes, which had been an Allen trademark for decades, his "new" style showed a greater subtlety of expression. In "Love Is Just Around the Corner," for instance, he follows good solos by Higginbotham, Marty Napoleon, Bailey, and Everett Barksdale; but his own contribution is unique and miles above theirs. He sighs and sings, using valve and lip slurs, growls and buzzes with the audacity of a master, making his solo not so much a succession of notes as a succession of moods. Even in a banal selection such as "Ride, Red, Ride," where Bailey and Hawkins are reduced to rolling triplets, Allen's swinging asymmetry commands attention. In "I Cover the Waterfront," taken at a medium-slow ballad tempo in which many jazzmen turn to mush, Red holds one's interest with lip shakes, tempo doubling, and that marvelous singing quality. This is not merely a five-star album, but one for the ages.

Also during the 1950s, three singers of the previous decade achieved their greatest fame. First of these was Newark-born **Sarah Vaughan** (1924–1990); the second was Chick Webb's former vocalist **Ella Fitzgerald** (1918–); the third was **Mel Tormé** (1925–). All three represented, in varying degrees, a new brand of jazz singer—the vocal virtuoso whose voice wasn't nasal, acidic, guttural, or in any way "illegitimate," but as beautifully produced as a classical singer's and as skillfully used as a jazz horn. The differences among them lay primarily in their vocal ranges, which in turn dictated their treatment of the music.

First, Vaughan. After singing with the big bands of Earl Hines and Billy Eckstine in the 1940s, the Divine Sarah struck out on a solo career. At first she went strictly pop, even waxing semiclassical numbers such as "The Lord's Prayer," but as she found her jazz wings, her spirit flew. Vaughan possessed a creamy, rich contralto not unlike Marian Anderson's. Like Anderson, she also had a flicker vibrato, which (in her early days) she controlled with perfect ease. Since her tone was luscious and warm, not unlike that of a tenor saxophone, she tended toward long lines, ballads, and the like. Her up-tempo numbers were scatted, though rarely. Most of the time Vaughan would improvise while singing the lyrics, something few others (besides Mel Tormé) have perfected. The following album, which catches her in her impressive prime, is a perfect example:

> *Sarah Vaughan*/Lullaby of Birdland; He's My Guy; April in Paris; Jim; You're Not the Kind; It's Crazy; Embraceable You; September Song; I'm Glad There Is You. EmArcy EXPR-1009/814 641-2 (LP/CD).

Here Vaughan is accompanied by Clifford Brown, tenor saxist Paul Quinichette, flautist Herbie Mann, pianist Jimmy Jones, bassist Joe Benjamin, and drummer Roy Haynes. This is an interesting lineup, with a Kansas City swing man (Quinichette), two boppers (Benjamin and Haynes), a West Coast cool player (Mann), and Brown, who pulls them all together in stylistic harmony.

Ella Fitzgerald never had Vaughan's warm, sensuous tone; hers was a bright, well-focused, yet sometimes hard high soprano, a jazz version of Lily Pons. Fitzgerald's command of the upper register was especially striking, her extreme high notes being taken in "head" voice. The amazing thing is that, unlike Vaughan, Fitzgerald never had formal voice training. What she did, she did instinctively and wonderfully well.

Also unlike Vaughan, Fitzgerald scatted a lot. In this respect she was closer in sound and style to a bop clarinetist, as opposed to Vaughan's tenor sax. Appropriately enough, Fitzgerald was much more at home in an up-tempo. Thus, where Vaughan could make magic with "Embraceable You," "Jim," and "I'm Glad There Is You," Fitzgerald produced classics with "How High the Moon," "Mr. Paganini," and "Please Don't Talk About Me When I'm Gone." In the following albums, one must in fairness point out the wonderfully underrated playing of her pianist and musical director, Paul Smith, one of the very few white players to tackle the virtuosic style of Tatum:

> *Compact Jazz: Ella Fitzgerald*/Mack the Knife; Desafinado; Mr. Paganini; I Can't Get Started; A Night in Tunisia; A-Tisket, A-Tasket; Shiny Stockings; Smooth Sailing; Goody Goody; Rough Ridin'; The Boy from Ipanema; Sweet Georgia Brown; Duke's Place; Misty; Somebody Loves Me; and How High the Moon. Verve 831 367-2/4 (CD/Cs).

> *A Perfect Match: Ella and Basie*/Please Don't Talk About Me When I'm Gone; St. Louis Blues; Sweet Georgia Brown; Some Other Spring; Fine and Mellow; Make Me Rainbows; 'Round Midnight; Honeysuckle Rose; You've Changed; and Basella. Pablo D/PACD/D5-2312-110 (LP/CD/Cs).

Mel Tormé was (and remains) slightly different from any other jazz singer, and so must be discussed separately. He possesses a baritone range with a tenor timbre, a natural limitation that gives his voice the veiled quality that has earned him the moniker "The Velvet Fog." (It is interesting to note that in his early years with the bands of Chico Marx and Artie Shaw, his range was higher—and as a result the "velvet" quality was considerably less.) Like Vaughan, he strayed from jazz to make a name for himself, in such songs as "County Fair." Once established, however, he spent less and less time in the pop field and more and more time in jazz.

Because of the unique nature of his voice, Tormé is best in ballads, though his improvising ability is second to none. The clear color of the voice, however, makes its impact on the ear as an essentially "cool" instrument—as in the following album, accompanied by Benny Barth, the Count Basie

Orchestra, and the cool-bop sounds of Shorty Rogers's Giants and the Marty Paich Dektette:

> *'Round Midnight*/I've Got the World on a String; Quiet Nights of Quiet Stars; Comin' Home, Baby; Sidney's Soliloquy; Dat Dere; When Sunny Gets Blue; Li'l Darlin'; Fascinating Rhythm; Four Brothers; Lonely Girl; Bluesette; That Face/Look at That Face; Gone With the Wind; That Old Feeling; Don't Let the Moon Get Away; All I Need is the Girl; I'll Be Seeing You; Lulu's Back in Town; When the Sun Comes Out; The Lady is a Tramp; Hello, Young Lovers; A Foggy Day; Porgy and Bess Medley; Hey, Look Me Over; The Surrey with the Fringe on Top; The Lady's in Love With You; and 'Round Midnight. Stash ST-CD-4 (CD).

Meanwhile, after a long period during which he fell from grace (as did any number of prebop musicians), Edward Kennedy Ellington came roaring back to prominence with a blockbuster showing at the 1956 Newport Jazz Festival. The particular hero was tenor saxist Paul Gonsalves, who swung through thirty-two choruses of Ellington's 1937 composition "Diminuendo and Crescendo in Blue" (see Chapter 4), resulting in a new Ellington contract (and lease on life) with Columbia Records. Bucking all trends while still leading them, Ellington's band was neither bop nor cool, though the addition of players such as Willie "Cat" Anderson (the highest trumpeter in history), hard-swing drummer Sam Woodyard, bop-cool cornetist Clark Terry, and airy-toned Gonsalves gave him different, more modern voices to work with. The fruit of Ellington's labor (in collaboration with Billy Strayhorn) to celebrate his new record deal was *Such Sweet Thunder*—the jazziest and most successful of all the "suites" Duke had written since *Black, Brown and Beige* in 1943:

> *Such Sweet Thunder*/Such Sweet Thunder; Sonnet for Caesar; Lady Mac; Sonnet to Hank Cinq; The Telecasters; Sonnet in Search of a Moor; Up and Down, Up and Down; Sonnet for Sister Kate; Half the Fun; The Star-Crossed

Lovers; Madness in Great Ones; and Circle of Fourths. Columbia Special Products JCL-1033 (LP).

In his "suite" years, Ellington had a tendency to be pretentious, both in his compositional forms and his titles. In this one, the latter is certainly in evidence, but *Such Sweet Thunder*'s lasting value is that the music can (and should) be enjoyed without even bothering with the titles. The liner notes go over all sorts of intended connections with Shakespeare's plays, none of which is necessary to enjoy the music. By and large, Ellington's inspiration seems to have been musical motifs, not literary ones. The classical hand of Bill Strayhorn is very much in evidence, and indeed it is almost impossible to tell which music was composed by whom (though I'd definitely give Ellington the funky, swaggering opening number).

Pretentiousness, unfortunately, was not a trait one could ascribe only to Ellington. The 1950s gave rise to the increasing classicalization of jazz, to the point where formality of structure threatened to overtake spontaneity of expression. The essential element of jazz—what was called, by *New Yorker* critic Whitney Balliett, "the sound of surprise"—was dissected and emasculated, not only by certain performers but by academics as well. Jazz met the classroom, and out of it came two generations of musicians with degrees as long as your arm but no real experience where it counted: on the field of battle.

With Morton, Beiderbecke, Raeburn, and Monk, one witnessed a true "third stream" in which artists well versed in the vocabulary of improvisation sought to expand their horizons by incorporating some classical elements. But with the next two groups under discussion, classically trained musicians sought to expand *their* vocabularies by incorporating jazz elements. Both had moments of success, yet both were ultimately self-defeating in their approach.

The **Modern Jazz Quartet**, or MJQ, had at least the ad-

vantage of in-field experience. Pianist **John Lewis** (1920–)
and drummer **Kenny Clarke** (1914–1985), the group's co-
founders, had been there in the early-to-mid-1940s when the
new music first took root, and both contributed greatly to its
sound. But paradoxically, their work with the MJQ tended
to be the most classicized of all. As is often the case with
groups of this sort, their first few years represented an amal-
gamation of something fresh and new and resulted in their
finest recorded performances. These showed a linear interplay by the four instruments, which rounded out with **Milt
Jackson** (1923–) on vibes and **Percy Heath** on bass, that
hadn't been consciously attempted by any previous group:

> *Django/*The Queen's Fancy; Delaunay's Dilemma; Milano;
> Autumn in New York; But Not for Me; Django; One Bass
> Hit; and La Ronde Suite. Prestige OJC/OJCCD-057 (LP/
> CD).

On this album, "The Queen's Fancy" is purposely classical
in sound and execution, and "La Ronde Suite" is a string of
four pieces in which each of the MJQ's members are given
solo prominence. In 1955, Connie Kay replaced Clarke on
drums, and the rhythm became more subtle, subdued, sophisticated, and slick. The records made with Kay are, on
the whole, unimpressive.

Exactly the opposite happened with the quartet founded
by pianist **Dave Brubeck** (1920–). A prominent member of
West Coast cool, he had worked in his early years with vibist/
drummer **Cal Tjader** (1925–1982), with whom he formed a
trio. But Tjader was gaining prominence on his own, so when
Brubeck formed his first quartet in 1952, with alto saxist **Paul
Desmond** (1924–1977)—a player strongly influenced by Lester Young and Lee Konitz—he used Ron Crotty on bass
and Lloyd Wright on drums. In 1954 Bob Bates and Joe
Dodge replaced Crotty and Wright, and the Brubeck Quartet
switched affiliations, from Fantasy to Columbia Records. The
big push was on.

Since Brubeck had almost single-handedly created the jazz

college circuit, Columbia capitalized on that with the album *Jazz Goes to College*. That record shows Brubeck evolving his highly personal style, and Desmond already in command of his, but the rhythm section was plodding, almost leaden, which left all the work up to the two lead voices. In 1957 drummer **Joe Morello** (1928–   ), whose brilliant work with Art Pepper was already well known, became the first non-West Coaster to join the group. His style, making the drums an integral part of the continuing evolvement of the music, represented a breakthrough. Indeed, Morello has survived as the finest drummer in the period between Roach and Elvin Jones. The album released that year, *Jazz Goes to Junior College*, marks the first real period of greatness for the quartet.

A fair comparison would be the two extended blues that open each of the two albums: "Balcony Rock" (1954) and "Bru's Blues" (1957). On the first, the entire success of the piece (such as it is) rests squarely on Desmond's shoulders, an uninspired Brubeck playing a series of block chords and clusters that go nowhere. On the latter, greater participation results from the interplay of Desmond, Brubeck, and Morello, with the drummer accenting off-rhythms strongly during the alto solo and pushing Brubeck on to marvelous heights in his solo. At that time, Bob Bates's brother Norman had replaced him on bass, but that, too, was a temporary assignment.

The real breakthrough came a year later, when Eugene Wright took over. Now Brubeck had three magnificent solo voices to work with, and the strain of doing most of the rhythm work himself was taken off. Their next few years together represented a culmination of all that had gone before, with an even greater dimension in asymmetrical time signatures. What Monk had hinted at, Brubeck finished. This album was their greatest achievement:

> *Time Out*/Blue Rondo à la Turk; Strange Meadow Lark; Take Five; Three to Get Ready; Kathy's Waltz; Every-

body's Jumpin'; and Pick Up Sticks. CBS CJ/CK/CJT-
40585 (LP/CD/Cs).

The tempi of the various pieces above bear consideration.
"Blue Rondo" is in 9/8, the most remote from jazz, counted
not as 3-3-3 but as 2-2-2-3. "Strange Meadow Lark" is in 4/
4 but includes some time-stretching elements within its ten-
bar theme. "Take Five" is in 5/4, counted as 3-2. "Three to
Get Ready" alternates between 4/4 and 3/4, while "Kathy's
Waltz" starts in 4, only later breaking into quick waltz tempo.
"Everybody's Jumpin' " and "Pick Up Sticks" are in 6/4. These
and other tempo variations continue to influence jazz even
today, though not as much as one might like.

For some bizarre reason, "Take Five" became a Top Ten
hit in 1960—the last time any pure jazz record did until
Ramsey Lewis's "Hang On, Sloopy" in 1966. Because of this,
and some truly ludicrous statements by Columbia's annota-
tors Steve Race and Mort Goode attributing all sorts of jazz
"firsts" to Brubeck that he didn't deserve, many self-righteous
jazz critics dismissed his real accomplishments and instead
praised the MJQ as harbingers of the future. But Brubeck,
Desmond, and Morello didn't really have to worry. Their
playing was appreciated by Hawkins, Parker, and one of jazz's
great geniuses, **Charles Mingus** (1922–1979).

Mingus was originally trained as a classical musician, and
in the mid-1940s was trying to originate a classical composers'
workshop in and around New York. Yet he became fasci-
nated with the new jazz of Parker, Gillespie, and Powell, and
by 1951 was one of the new mainstream's greatest bass players. In 1956 and 1957, inspired by the Brubeck Quartet's
rhythmic innovations, he turned his allegiance to a *jazz* composers' workshop.

Mingus's stated intention was to declassicalize the contemporary jazz experience, which he felt had gotten too far away
from Ellington and Morton (two of his idols). Yet Mingus
was so great a composer and orchestrator, creating loose yet

dense structures where the soloists could improvise freely
while still contributing to the whole, that his pieces became
vignettes frozen in time—cool-bop counterparts to Morton's
Red Hot Peppers. This is not to denigrate his music—one
could scarcely do so to such works of lasting value in any
case—but to explain how his intent was counteracted by his
actions. His greatest achievement was in teaching saxist Dan-
nie Richmond to play drums in a manner similar to Morello,
thus freeing himself and his players from rhythmic con-
straints. These three albums sum up Mingus's achievements:

> *Mingus Ah Um*/Better Git It in Your Soul; Goodbye Pork
> Pie Hat; Boogie Stop Shuffle; Self-Portrait in Three
> Colors; Open Letter to Duke; Bird Calls; Fables of Faubus;
> Pussy Cat Dues; and Jelly Roll. CBS CJ/CK/CJT-40648
> (LP/CD/Cs).

> *Mingus at Antibes*/Wednesday Night Prayer Meeting;
> Prayer for Passive Resistance; What Love?; I'll Remember
> April; Folk Forms I; and Better Git It in Your Soul. At-
> lantic 90532-1/2/4 (LP/CD/Cs).

> *The Black Saint and the Sinner Lady*/Solo Dancer; Duet Solo
> Dancers; Group Dancers; Trio and Group Dancers; Single
> Solos and Group Dance; and Group and Solo Dance. MCA
> Impulse! MCA/MCAD/MCAC-5649 (LP/CD/Cs).

The structural and coloristic diversity of Mingus's concep-
tions are readily in evidence here. His music is so orchestrally
dense that it often sounds as if there are many more musicians
on these sides than there really are. In the first album we
hear his compatriots of the late 1950s, such as saxists John
Handy and Shafi Hadi and trombonist Jimmy Knepper. In
the second we hear trumpeter Ted Curson and the alto sax
and bass clarinet of **Eric Dolphy** (1928–1964), a strange but
important transitional figure who greatly influenced John
Coltrane later. Dolphy tried to include atonal excursions, à
la Schoenberg, in his improvisations. To some extent he suc-
ceeded, but he never learned that you couldn't make this
work unless you create a chord progression that goes some-

where logically and/or have your accompanying musicians follow you into these new musical realms. Dolphy was heavily criticized for being unable to improvise properly on a chord pattern, whereas what he really needed (as can be heard here in "Wednesday Night Prayer Meeting" and "I'll Remember April") was someone to alter the chording underneath him. This was something Mingus, with his infallible ear and quick mind, could do quite easily.

In *The Black Saint and the Sinner Lady*, Mingus gave us jazz's first great "concept" album, one that could not (or at least *should* not) be excerpted simply because the whole is greater than the sum of its parts. The music is interrelated in a way similar to, yet less pretentiously than, the music dramas of Richard Wagner. It was perhaps fitting that the original liner notes were written not by a musician, but by a psychologist! One of the problems that contemporary musicians and critics had with Mingus was that his music penetrated *too* deeply into one's feelings. Like the late quartets of Beethoven, it was simply too intense for its time.

Today Mingus's music has lost none of its freshness and impact, but in its day record companies were afraid to release it for fear of poor sales. RCA has long been chastised for holding back the album *Tijuana Moods* five years before release, but Atlantic was just as guilty in the case of *The Clown*, recorded in 1957 but not released until 1961; and *Mingus at Antibes*, recorded "live" in 1960, waited *sixteen years* before Atlantic decided to issue it!

The experiments of Mingus and Brubeck did not go unheeded, however. They were assimilated into the music of the next generation, which almost ended the popularity of jazz as we knew it.

7.
New Times, New Sounds

As President Eisenhower ended his second term of office, jazz was entering its seventh decade of existence. Jazz had already evolved from music for dancing to music for listening (and studying), but—with some exceptions—the upcoming decade would prove a fruitless one for its further evolution. Part of the problem came from its new elitism, wherein concert halls and college campuses became equal partners with nightclubs and dancc halls as peiformance places. Another was that the college audience was changing, too. Bob Dylan had given folk music its conscience back, and the tremendous social upheavals of the sixties turned the former collge audience toward songs with a meaning, both in folk and rock. But the real stumbling block to evolution was the direction in which the musicians themselves were taking jazz: away from a steady rhythm of any sort and toward something so anarchistic and confused that jazz lost most of its audience.

There were few signs of this at the beginning of the decade, when things were still moving well. A new vocal group had just come into prominence that would revolutionize their function in jazz. This was the trio of **Dave Lambert** (1917–1966), **Jon Hendricks** (1921–), and **Annie Ross** (1930–), known by their last names only. Their aesthetics were as far removed from the Boswell Sisters as the Boswells were from previous groups. Though they sang in harmony at times and used some crossover chording, they more often sang in counterpoint to each other, like three jazz horns. This was especially helped by the pure, high voice of Annie Ross, who sadly left the group in 1963. The following album made for Columbia, with Ike Isaacs's trio, solidified their reputation:

> *Everybody's Boppin'*/Charleston Alley; Moanin'; Twisted; Centerpiece; Bijou; Cloudburst; Gimme That Wine; Everybody's Boppin'; Sermonette; Summertime; Home Cookin'; Blue; Come on Home; Cottontail; and Midnight Indigo. CBS CJ/CK/CJT-45020 (LP/CD/Cs).

As can be seen from the above titles, a good part of their style involved the giving of lyrics to formerly instrumental pieces, a practice known as "vocalese": Charlie Barnet's "Charleston Alley," Wardell Gray's "Twisted," and Woody Herman's "Bijou" are three of the best examples. This little trick has been picked up on and enhanced by such diverse talents as Mel Tormé, the Pointer Sisters, and Manhattan Transfer, and is so commonplace today that one forgets it is a relatively recent invention.

Meanwhile, Miles Davis, after a long period of experimentation, had come up with a highly inventive, progressive group. It included, in addition to the leader's trumpet, alto saxist Julian "Cannonball" Adderly, tenor saxist John Coltrane, bassist Paul Chambers, pianist Red Garland (later Bill Evans), and drummer Jimmy Cobb. They gave concerts and made records together that firmly established them as the best contemporary jazz group.

Adderly was a hard-bop saxist whose ideas soon carried him to the forefront of the jazz world. Cobb and Chambers were two gifted rhythm men whose role in the group has been sadly neglected. Bill Evans, the only white member, was a highly introspective pianist influenced by Powell and Brubeck. And Coltrane, as every good jazz buff knows, became the fourth (and last) great legend of the music. He took the linear playing of Sonny Rollins and expanded it into something very personal, though debatable in quality. But we'll cross that bridge when we come to it.

The watershed album for Davis's sextet was *Kind of Blue*, a series of five pieces, none of which the group had played prior to recording and most of which were first takes. Its influence on other musicians, in its multilinear improvisations, can hardly be overstated:

> *Kind of Blue*/So What?; Freddie Freeloader; Blue in Green; Flamenco Sketches; and All Blues. CBS CJ/CK/CJT-40579 (LP/CD/Cs).

Again, like Brubeck and the MJQ, the Davis group was heavy on formal structure. "So What?" is a theme based on sixteen bars of one scale, eight of another, and eight of the first. "Freddie Freeloader" (on which pianist Wynton Kelly replaced Evans) is a twelve-measure blues, and "Blue in Green" is a ten-measure circular form played in various augmenting and diminution of time values. "Flamenco Sketches" is a 6/8, twelve-bar blues. "All Blues," conversely, isn't a blues at all but a series of five scales, each to be played as long as the soloist wishes until he completes the series.

This concept of modal structure—a preset arrangement of the eight notes in a scale—was to influence jazz for years to come. No matter that not all musicians could do it coherently; once the idea took root and the jazz critics idealized it, it became mandatory for any new group to tackle at least one modal piece in order to be accepted. Ironically, many critics saw modal development as something that allowed the soloist greater freedom. They either ignored or never saw the inherent pitfalls, where solos eventually got so long and loose that coherency and structure collapsed.

Curiously, a different modal concept was being evolved and brought to fruition at about the same time. This was the

Lydian Chromatic Concept, worked out by composer/arranger **George Russell** (1923–). It used an entirely new system of tonality based on the Lydian scale, which is based on the fourth degree and dates back to ancient Greek music. By contrast, Russell's music was actually freer and less constraining than the Davis mode; the soloists could improvise in or around the underlying chord structure in any manner they saw fit. The following album introduced Russell's new world to jazz:

> *New York, N.Y. & Jazz in the Space Age*/Manhattan; Big City Blues; Manhatta-Rico; East Side Medley; A Helluva Town; Chromatic Universe; Dimensions; The Lydiot; and Waltz from Outer Space. MCA 4017 (two LPs; *New York, N.Y.* available alone on MCAD-31371, CD).

The reader will note the presence, here, of several musicians already mentioned: Art Farmer, Max Roach, Jon Hendricks, John Coltrane, and Bill Evans (the last-named a particular favorite of Russell's), in addition to Doc Severinsen. Russell exhibited a funkier feel and greater sense of humor in his music, which led to a remarkably relaxed atmosphere. Surprisingly, his music was "over the head" of most lay listeners and so never achieved the stranglehold on recordings of the 1960s that the Davis mode did.

There were, though, two new groups who only dabbled briefly in the murky waters of modality. The first of these, and less well remembered, was the **Toshiko-Mariano Quartet**. This was the musically fruitful, if personally unhappy, meshing of two of jazz's loners—pianist **Toshiko Akiyoshi** (1929–) and alto saxist **Charlie Mariano** (1923–)—with bassist Gene Cherico and drummer Eddie Marshall. Their playing, like that of Davis's sextet, took established styles in new directions. But Davis was with Columbia, Toshiko-Mariano were with Nat Hentoff's little label Candid, so the distribution and dissemination of their marvelous music was more limited.

Akiyoshi, the successor to Mary Lou Williams as the greatest female jazz musician, began as a stylistic pupil of Bud Powell but soon blossomed into a unique original. She played, then, with a lot of time-stretching and tone clusters. Her own compositions, discussed in more detail later, were based on the Oriental music of her childhood, though heavily filtered through bop. Mariano, a veteran of Stan Kenton's orchestra, was an extremely talented player whose work still has not gotten its just due. An obvious descendant of Parker, Mariano likewise worked at developing his own voice. That he found it by the time he recorded with Toshiko is evidenced in the following album:

> *Toshiko-Mariano Quartet*/When You Meet Her; Little T; Toshiko's Elegy; Deep River; and Long Yellow Road. Candid CCD-79012 (available from DA Music, [404] 977- 4172).

The one concession of Toshiko-Mariano to modality, "Little T," is handled far more intelligently and cohesively than most of those who followed in the footsteps of Davis's sextet. Otherwise this is a wide-open blowing date, with Akiyoshi and Mariano spurring each other on to tremendous heights. The two Akiyoshi originals, "Long Yellow Road" and "Toshiko's Elegy," preface by almost twelve years her writing for her big band. The former was later transcribed to full score, while "Elegy," a jazz samba, was reworked into "Warning: Success May Be Hazardous to Your Health." Truly, then, these are landmark recordings, as much for what they state as for what they portend.

The other great combo of the period was a direct offshoot of Davis's sextet, the Bill Evans Trio. For nearly a year, **Bill Evans** (1929–1983) worked at close quarters with young bassist Scott La Faro and drummer Paul Motian at solidifying the musical avenues initially explored with Davis. In Evans's mind, the modal technique was to be approached tastefully and occasionally. He was much more concerned with time, tone color, and the interrelationships of the instruments in the trio. His work with La Faro and Motian was a natural extension of the Brubeckian style and worked brilliantly, as witnessed on following album:

Sunday at the Village Vanguard/Gloria's Step; Solar; Alice in Wonderland; My Man's Gone Now; All of You; and Jade Visions. Riverside/Fantasy OJC/OJCCD-140 (LP/CD).

Why didn't the Evans Trio exert a greater influence? Two reasons. First, Evans was white, and the new social consciousness of the sixties ascribed all of jazz's greatest developments to black players. Jazz historians such as LeRoi Jones and Marshall Stearns did their best to eliminate as much white influence as possible in their books. Second, young La Faro was killed in an auto crash in early July 1961. Evans retired from jazz, coming out only to make an occasional record to support his heroin habit. Not until the early seventies, when he formed a new group with bassist Eddie Gomez and drummer Marty Morell, did he again find partners on the same level:

Bill Evans: The Tokyo Concert/Mornin' Glory; Up With the Lark; Yesterday I Heard the Rain; My Romance; T.T.T.T.; When Autumn Comes; Hullo Bolinas; Gloria's Step; and Green Dolphin Street. Fantasy 9160-9457/ OJCCD-345-2 (LP/CD).

Comparing both albums, one finds that the differences aren't nearly as striking as the similarities. Though Gomez was an even stronger and more audacious bassist than La Faro, the tradition is continued; in fact, Evans and Gomez pay La Faro the ultimate compliment by performing his original work "Gloria's Step." The immediate connection between the two Bill Evans trios is so strong that one could easily imagine the second following the first by just two or three years rather than ten.

The man who most influenced the 1960s, however, was tenor saxist **John Coltrane** (1926–1967), the fourth and last great legend in jazz. (It should be noted that legendary status does not necessarily indicate greater creativity, though in the case of Beiderbecke and Parker that was certainly true; all it means is that these figures were lionized by peripheral jazz fans more than their fellows.) Coltrane was that jazz rarity, a late bloomer; even at age thirty, in 1956, his playing was standard bop style, not even as forward-looking as that of Sonny Rollins. Coltrane left Miles Davis temporarily and spent a year working with Thelonious Monk, who taught him an entirely new concept of rhythm and melodic construction. By the time he rejoined Davis, Coltrane had begun to play note clusters and those downward-winding passages that became known as "snakes."

After leaving Davis in 1959, Coltrane began experimenting with chords on the tenor sax—not breathing one note while playing another, but actual harmonics of a third. He also began to experiment on the soprano sax at the encouragement of Eric Dolphy, which he claimed gave him "a different voice," and working on rapid bursts and squeals, which he called "sheets of sound." He explored twelve-tone rows and East Indian music, in which chords remain unchanged for many minutes while the soloist improvises in whatever key or keys he wishes. This in turn led to his recording a great deal of material, with groups large and small, bearing African or East Indian names.

If all this sounds somewhat confusing or chaotic, it was; when he applied Eastern modes to his 1961 recording of Rodgers and Hammerstein's song "My Favorite Things," his integrity as a jazzman was questioned. Shortly after recording the album *Crescent* in 1964, Coltrane went off the deep end, his last three years spent in an ever-increasing ruckus of confused harmonies and rhythms. Nevertheless, when he played with pianist **McCoy Tyner** (1938–) and drummer **Elvin Jones** (1927–), both of whom were superb musicians who could play two different rhythms simultaneously yet remain coherent, Coltrane's playing was outstanding. These two albums represent his best work:

Coltrane Jazz/Little Old Lady; Village Blues; My Shining Hour; Fifth House; Harmonique; Like Sonny; I'll Wait and Pray; and Some Other Blues. Atlantic SD-1354/1354-2 (LP/CD).

John Coltrane Quartet: Coltrane/Out of This World; Tunji; Soul Eyes; The Inch Worm; and Miles' Mode. MCA/Impulse! MCA/MCAD/MCAC-5883 (LP/CD/Cs).

The first album, most of which was recorded with Wyn Kelly on piano and Jimmy Cobb on drums, is closer to his work with the Davis group. "Little Old Lady," in fact, is done in a surprisingly happy, swinging style, very unlike most of his later output. "Fifth House" is also quite upbeat, ending with an example of his chord playing. This technique greatly influenced Rahsaan Roland Kirk and is heard to even finer advantage in "Harmonique." On the second album, his playing gets a little chaotic toward the end of "Out of This World"; still, most of it is pretty interesting.

Sadly, Coltrane's experimentation in what became known as "free jazz," or jazz without any firm rhythmic or harmonic base, influenced the growing trend of complexity for complexity's sake. Nor was Coltrane alone; avant-garde pianist **Cecil Taylor** (1933–), who had been experimenting with free jazz since the mid-1950s, is the single most controversial figure in jazz history. Critics almost universally love him for what they describe as "harmonic daring" and "astonishing technique," while audiences are generally confused or hostile. Taylor, who came from the world of modern classical music to jazz, ostensibly applies the same principles to his music that classical composers Krzysztof Penderecki and Karlheinz Stockhausen apply to theirs. But in the density of a jazz performance, all Taylor really sounds like is a seven-year-old flipping his fingers randomly, tunelessly, and noisily over the keyboard. All of this "free jazz" eventually led, in the mid-1960s, to the Albert Ayler Trio. Ayler, a tenor/soprano saxist who followed in the footsteps of Taylor and Coltrane, created jazz which was all but chaos on vinyl, though he, too, exerted a great influence on those who followed.

While Coltrane and Ayler were taking jazz into the deep and murky waters of random (or chance) tonality, yet another saxist was refining and redefining the sparse style of Paul Desmond. This was **Ornette Coleman** (1930–), whose pianoless trio explored what he called "harmolodics": improvising on the melody, harmony, and rhythm simultaneously. This concept was scarcely new to jazz: Tatum did it in the 1930s and Mingus in the 1950s. Yet Coleman's group managed to sound less "classicized" than the latter. His sparse, unemotional playing drew as much criticism as praise, and the group's style was, eventually, limiting. Nevertheless, for a few years they were an island of enjoyable stasis in a sea of musical restlessness, as the following album shows:

At the "Golden Circle" Stockholm/Faces and Places; Dee Dee; European Echoes; and Dawn. Blue Note BST/CDP/4BT-84224-2 (LP/CD/Cs).

In many ways, this period in jazz bore an unhappy resemblance to what was happening in classical music. Players were getting away from trying to communicate with their listeners, instead pursuing intellectual exercises. In some cases, the majority of listeners (and even some critics) questioned the very structure under which they operated, since one group's style was often incompatible with everybody else's. During the late 1960s and early 1970s, with many being fed up with the modal, Eastern, and chaotic influences in jazz, two things happened. First, reactionaries appeared—only this time, instead of in New Orleans style, they were in swing and bop style. Second, in a pathetic effort to make jazz "popular," many performers started cranking out a brand of R&B-pop-funk with a jazz flavor, which was soon dubbed "fusion."

The most prominent of the former was the rather conventional piano-bass-drums trio led by Chicago-born **Ramsey Lewis** (1935–). A classically trained pianist, Lewis bypassed the classical complexities of both the "cool" MJQ style and the "soulful" one of Mingus. There was absolutely nothing fancy about Lewis's playing, or that of his sidemen: This was straight-ahead gospel-soul jazz in the tradition of Eddie Heywood and Erroll Garner. Because of their penchant for playing jazz versions of popular "hit" songs, such as "The 'In' Crowd" and "Hang On, Sloopy," they gained an astonishing amount of fame at a time when Coltrane and Coleman were hawking their convoluted, complex wares. Because of this, there has been a tendency to ignore or belittle the Ramsey Lewis Trio. But make no mistake: They were a kickin', swingin' little outfit. Bassist Eldee Young and drummer Red Holt laid down a solid beat, based on late-swing and hard-bop principles; Lewis could really "preach" on the piano, and the classical background of all three gave them a penchant for both well-constructed performances and judicious use of dynamics. Their crescendos and diminuendos were as well or better executed than any other group in jazz history, as heard on the following album:

> *The Greatest Hits of Ramsey Lewis*/The "In" Crowd; My Babe; Since I Fell for You; Something You Got; A Hard Day's Night; Hang On, Sloopy; The Caves; Dancing in the Street; Felicidade; Wade in the Water; Ain't That Peculiar?; Blues for the Night Owl; Function at the Junction; Lonely Avenue; 1-2-3; Look-a-Here; High Heel Sneakers; and Uptight (Everything's Alright). Chess CH2/CH2C/CHD-6021 (two LPs/two Cs/one CD).

Among the leaders of the latter group were some fine, bona fide jazzmen: pianist **Herbie Hancock** (1940–), who outsold all others in this field; **Young-Holt Unlimited**, a group made up of the Ramsey Lewis Trio's old rhythm section; trumpeter **Randy Brecker** (1945–), now back in jazz but at that time with Blood, Sweat & Tears; and even Miles Davis, who made a rather sad plea for attention with his *Bitches' Brew* album. Their work can be dismissed as far as providing any "new direction," since little came of it but creative stunting.

One of the few exceptions to the rule was **Return to Forever**, a superb jazz band that simply happened to be electric (as opposed to an electric funk band that dabbles in jazz). This was led by the brilliant pianist/composer **Armando "Chick" Corea** (1941–) and included such superb musicians as flutist/soprano saxist Joe Farrell, vocalist/percussionist Flora Purim, the brilliant young bassist Stanley Clarke, and especially drummer Airto Moreira, whose ability to play exceptionally complex rhythms exceeded even the abilities of Elvin Jones. Corea's firm foundation in classical music has, at times, led to music that can only tentatively be called jazz (though, one hastens to add, it is by no means bad music), but in Return to Forever he created a true jazz context that was airy, spacious, relaxing, and engaging to the mind all at the same time. Among its early successes was Corea's now-classic composition "Spain," but the following album may be truly said to represent the group's apex:

> *Return to Forever*/Return to Forever; Crystal Silence; What Game Shall We Play Today?; Sometime Ago; and La Fiesta. ECM 811978-1/2/4 (LP/CD/Cs).

The truest testament to their good taste—in textures, in their use of dynamics, and in their musical concept—is that this album still sounds completely modern some twenty years after it was made. Sadly, the delicate balance represented in their early work did not last. A change in record labels (and commercial potential) pushed up the volume, and before long the breath-stopping perfection of their playing was lost in a sea of rock guitars that gave the group "superstar" status while severely compromising their jazz content.

The only electrified fusion band to achieve true musical distinction was the **Brecker Brothers Band**, co-led by Randy and his sax-playing brother **Michael** (1949–). Perhaps it helped that they were just the right age, which is to say in their late twenties to early thirties, to be both well-trained jazz musicians and properly tuned in to what was new in both the pop and modern jazz fields. Nevertheless, their mid-1970s band, which included such stalwarts of the "fusion" school as alto saxist David Sanborn, guitarists Steve Khan and Hiram Bullock, electric-pianist Paul Schaffer, and bassist Will Lee, played a style that bound the heavy rock beat and synthesized sounds to truly creative jazz that *went* somewhere, rather than *staying* somewhere, as most such music does. In any event, the music they laid down in those now distant RCA studio sessions has remained a *locus classicus* of their kind; it's a shame that their former bandsmen aren't anywhere near as creative:

> *The Brecker Bros. Collection, Vol. 1*/Skunk Funk; Sponge; Squids; Funky Sea, Funky Dew; Inside Out; Dream Theme; I Don't Know Either; Bathsheba; Straphangin'; Threesome; and East River. RCA/Novus 3075-2/4-N (CD/ Cs).

At about the same time as these experiments were going on, one of the strangest and most unique of jazzmen was recording his last will and testament. This was the multi-talented **Rahsaan Roland Kirk** (1936–1977), a blind man who astonished the music world by his ability to play three instruments (tenor sax, manzello, and strich) simultaneously. Though he claimed (for the public's sake) to be able to breathe through his ears, the actual fact was that Kirk had the most highly developed circular breathing of any jazz instrumentalist who ever lived. This means that the player sucks in the air through his nose while blowing out his mouth;

pictures of Kirk in action do indeed show his nostrils splayed outward, and his cheeks puffed up like a hamster's. Still, Kirk was more than just a trickster. He was a creative, often tasteful musician who had roots in both the hard-bop styles of Dexter Gordon and Illinois Jacquet and the R&B styles of Louis Jordan and King Curtis. Kirk had led a rhythm and blues band at age fourteen, and its influence never left his musical style, though he progressed as an improvisor well beyond its limitations.

In addition to the above-mentioned instruments, Kirk also played trumpet, clarinet, flute, and nose flute. He could also sing and play the flute simultaneously, by blowing lightly over the flute mouthpiece while he sang. All of these gifts, including his compositional and arranging talents, went into the creation of the album many consider his masterpiece:

> *The Case of the Three-Sided Dream (in Color)*/Conversation; Bye Bye Blackbird; Horses; High-Heel Sneakers; Dream; Echoes of Primitive Ohio and and Chili Dogs; The Entertainer (Blues); Dream; Freaks for the Festival; Dream; Portrait of Those Beautiful Ladies; Dream; The Entertainer; Dream; Freaks for the Festival; sesroH; Bye Bye Blackbird; and Conversation. Atlantic SD-1674/1674-2 (two LPs/one CD).

In this album Kirk splices into his recurrent "dreams" such echoes of past jazz as Duke Ellington's "Creole Love Call" and snippets of Billie Holiday, Nat "King" Cole, and Charlie Parker; Kirk's trumpet-playing, specifically on "Bye Bye Blackbird," is eerily reminiscent of Miles Davis; and his tenor sax pays constant homage to his idols Byas and Jacquet. One of the album's highlights is his rearrangement of Scott Joplin's "The Entertainer" as a slow, funky blues—strangely enough, it works. Sadly, Kirk suffered a stroke shortly after this album was completed. He regained the use of one side of his body, and had learned to adjust his playing accordingly, but a second stroke cut him down in 1977. He was an odd original who influenced no one, but his uniqueness will be sorely missed.

On the other hand, some of the reactionaries, who included a handful of originals going for second careers, played some very interesting music. Primary among these in the big-band scene were cornetist **Thad Jones** (1923–) and drummer **Mel Lewis** (1929–1990), who founded a fine, Gil Evans-style bop-cool band. Like Evans, their music was transparent and airy despite a fairly large ensemble; unlike him, they swung a little harder, incorporating Latin rhythms and polyrhythms, and "layered" their sound much like a symphony orchestra. The following CD gives an excellent idea of what they were all about:

> *The Definitive Thad Jones, Vol. 2*/Second Race; Tip Toe; Don't Get Sassy; Rhoda Map; Cherry Juice. MusicMasters 5046-2-C.

Other reactionaries included trumpeter **Freddie Hubbard** (1942–) and **Ruby Braff** (1927–), the former an outstanding bop stylist in the Clifford Brown mold and the latter having played fine swing music since the late 1940s; tenor saxist **Scott Hamilton** (1950–), who plays in the Hawkins/Ben Webster mold; and alto saxist **Richie Cole** (1948–), a follower of Parker and Phil Woods. This era also saw a renewal of interest in singer Mel Tormé, drummer/bandleader Buddy Rich, and Brubeck, who had returned to jazz after years of mediocre classical compositions.

The most creative of those who tried a comeback was Toshiko Akiyoshi. Since her late-1960s marriage to a younger reactionary, tenor saxist/flutist **Lew Tabackin** (1944–), Akiyoshi had dreams of leading a big band to play her own compositions and arrangements. Dream became reality in 1972; the debut in 1974 on RCA of the **Akiyoshi-Tabackin Big Band** was hailed by Leonard Feather as a major arrival in jazz. But RCA wasn't interested in promoting anything that wasn't funk or fusion, so their records got little play, little push, and poor distribution. Even years later, after word had gotten around and jazz fans looked for them, Akiyoshi's RCA albums were seldom in the record bins.

Nevertheless, this is the most creative big band since Ellington's, one that carried his progressive swing through hard bop and Oriental influences. Now, in her orchestral work, Akiyoshi's Occidental roots showed through. Since Tabackin was not only her husband but also a powerhouse player whose circular breathing enabled him to cut choruses in one breath, there were also showcases for his talents (and *his* originals). The following albums give a fair sampling of their range:

The Toshiko Akiyoshi—Lew Tabackin Big Band/Studio J; American Ballad; Quadrille, Anyone?; Children in the Temple Ground; The First Night; Kogun; Since Perry/ Yet Another Tear; and Road Time Shuffle. RCA/Novus Series '70 3106-2-N (CD).

Tanuki's Night Out/Tanuki's Night Out; Yet Another Tear; Lament for Sonny; A Bit Byas'd; Falling Petal; and Lew's Theme. JAM 006 (LP,OP).

In the albums above, the Oriental influence is most strongly felt in "Kogun," "Tanuki's Night Out," and "Children in the Temple Ground." In these, Akiyoshi uses clarinets and flutes in the most unusual way since Ellington, to play Chinese and Japanese themes in a jazz context, while alto saxes bend and slur notes to simulate traditional Oriental instruments. These are even enhanced in "Kogun" by *kotsuzumi* and *ohysuzumi* players. The cumulative effect may seem bizarre at first, but musically it holds together. On the flip side, of course, are the boppish "Studio J" and "A Bit Byas'd," and the hard-rocking "Road Time Shuffle."

Another facet of jazz that received a much-needed boost during the 1970s was the art of jazz vocalization. With such artists as Fitzgerald, Vaughan, and Tormé still around but relegated to the scrap heap of "old-timers," it was time that new and exciting artists appeared on the scene to reawaken interest in this very difficult art. Ironically, one of those "new" artists was one who had been around almost as long as Tormé and Vaughan. The difference was, no one in America knew about her: She was British, and she had been out of jazz for years, pursuing a solo career as a pop and Broadway singer.

This was Clementina Dinah Campbell, better known as **Cleo Laine** (1927–   ). Her debut at New York's Carnegie Hall in 1972 was a revelation: Here was a female jazz singer with the growling low range of a Bessie Smith, a hip rhythmic sense that could compete with Anita O'Day, and a high range that could out-Ella Ella. Laine's husband, saxist/bandleader Johnny Dankworth, was in a large measure responsible for her musical success. As a disciple of both Johnny Hodges and Charlie Parker, he managed to synthesize Hodges's purity of tone with Parker's angularity of line to produce a style that was, in the 1950s, quite unique; but like Cleo Laine herself, he was scarcely known outside Britain.

As both her husband and musical director, Dankworth brought Cleo back to jazz via tightly arranged vignettes designed to show off her range. Critics have at times attacked her for the premeditated condition of her improvisations, but as we have seen, this is scarcely an argument against her work being jazz. More to the point, she has often reverted to a purely pop environment; it makes her more money but compromises the quality of her work. The following album, however, is both a fine example of her live "act" and more of a jazz than a pop excursion:

> *Cleo at Carnegie*/Any Place I Hang My Hat; It's a Grand Night for Singing; Good Morning; It's a Lovely Day Today; I'm Shadowing You; Crazy Rhythm; Primrose Color Blue; We Are the Music Makers; You Spotted Snakes; Methuselah; When I Was One and Twenty; Sing Me No Song; Triboro Fair; You've Got to Do What You've Got to Do; He Was Beautiful; Turkish Delight; Never Let Me Go; Georgia on My Mind; Lazy Bones; The Nearness

of You; I Get Along Without You Very Well; My Resistance Is Low; Stardust; and I Want to Be Happy. DRG DARC2/DARC2C/CDXP-2101 (two LPs/Cs, one CD).

The second great jazz singer of this period was an American black man, **Al Jarreau** (1941–). Though his music had, even from the beginning, trace elements of fusion, one instantly forgave him for the sheer virtuosity and *joie de vivre* with which he sang. Jarreau's voice was a high, untrained tenor, with superb command of coloration and a glib-tongued technique that enabled him to rattle off rapid-fire improvisations with the accuracy and harmonic daring of, say, a trumpet or alto sax. Within a few years he was to be found drifting farther and farther away from jazz, and more and more into the murky seas of commercial funk and junk. In his case the defection is particularly frustrating because he is truly unique; fortunately, we still have records such as the following to remind us of how good he really was:

Look to the Rainbow/Letter Perfect; Rainbow in Your Eyes; One Good Turn; Could You Believe; Burst In With the Dawn; Better Than Anything; So Long Girl; Look to the Rainbow; You Don't See Me; Take Five; Loving You; and We Got By. Warner Bros. 2BZ/2Z5-3052; 3052-2 (two LPs/Cs, one CD).

On this album (and a few others as well), one can hear Jarreau's early preference in musical style: electronic keyboards playing long chords and delicate lines behind him, the occasional sprinkle of vibes and percussion, and a supple bass (these instruments played here by Tom Canning, Lynn Blessing, Joe Correro, and Abraham Laboriel). Against this gentle, slightly funky backdrop Jarreau would chant, cry, moan, or machine-gun his dazzling improvisations like so much scattershot against a soft cushion. The effect was mesmerizing, especially when combined with Jarreau's friendly, deceptively casual, yet intense stage appearance.

Toward the end of the 1970s, with pure jazz once more on an upswing of popularity, some former fusionists temporarily gave up that pursuit to play good music. Chief among these was the **V.S.O.P. Quintet,** founded in the late 1960s with Miles Davis, altoist Wayne Shorter, pianist Hancock, bassist Ron Carter, and drummer Tony Williams. In 1977 the same lineup, now with Freddie Hubbard on trumpet, toured and recorded to tremendous critical and public acclaim:

> *V.S.O.P.—The Quintet*/One of a Kind; Jessica; Dolores; Byrdlike; Lawra; Third Plane; Darts; and Little Waltz. CBS CGK-34976 (CD).

In brief, V.S.O.P.'s music was multirhythmic but never obtuse. It was also Hubbard's "coming out" period; though he had been around since the 1960s, he was finally recognized for the exciting, inventive player he is. Jazz lovers greeted V.S.O.P.'s arrival with a sigh of relief, and a standing ovation; the music seemed, at long last, to be back on track. But both Hubbard and Hancock took the fusion route. Hubbard returned to acoustic jazz, but Hancock apparently likes the extra money fusion brings. As a result, this album is looked on as a sort of watershed period for jazz; certainly few discs, before or since, have been as creative.

8.
Confirmation

As jazz nears its hundredth birthday, reactionism is the order of the day. Unlike the Moldy Fig movement of the 1940s, however, which dead-ended itself by retreating to pre-Morton forms instead of taking him one step farther, the modern reactionaries are exploring new corners and cracks in the music of the past—and jazz hasn't been as popular since Brubeck left the campus. Not that a record by Tania Maria or Wynton Marsalis will ever outsell Bon Jovi or Madonna; but it's getting a share of the market, bringing home the bucks, and (once again) largely acoustic.

Tania Maria (1944–   ), the Brazilian spitfire who burst on the American scene in 1981 with her album *Piquant,* is one of the principal catalysts in bringing rock fans into the jazz camp. Without condescending to rubbish, Tania Maria has transformed the rock beat into a heavy Latino-bop-African mode, over which her gutsy piano and flamboyant singing fly like the wind. Even in ballads, the churning undercurrent of rhythm never really comes to rest. She also, like Akiyoshi, writes a good deal of her own material. The one problem with Tania Maria is that so far she has shown little growth or change in style over five LPs; the following one, made in 1983, captures that style well:

Come With Me/Sangria; Embraceable You; Lost in Ama-
zonia; Sementes, Graines & Seeds; Come With Me; Nega;
It's All Over Now; and Euzinha. Concord Picante CJP-
200/CCD-4200/CJP-200-C (LP/CD/Cs).

Meanwhile, **Arthur Blythe**, an altoist with roots in both
R&B and the music of Monk, created a quintet unique in all
of jazz. Backing his wide-ranging and incredibly flexible sax
were guitarist Kelvyn Bell, cellist Abdul Wadud, drummer
Bobby Battle, and tuba player Bob Stewart. This richly tex-
tured, pianoless small band produced some of the most stim-
ulating, modern, and swinging music in that idiom since the
Mingus Jazz Workshop. They play mostly in ensemble, Blythe
being the principal soloist, their churning, strongly accented
counterpoint providing a fine foil. Occasional solos by Wadud
and Stewart show them as virtuosos, the former going up
into the viola range and the latter sometimes resembling a
French horn or trombone. Their music had a remarkable
joie de vivre, despite its harmonic and rhythmic complexity,
plus qualities of beckoning and surprise. In short, they were
the premiere small group of the early 1980s, as the following
LP amply demonstrates:

Elaborations/Elaboration; Metamorphosis; Sister Daisy;
One Mint Julep; Shadows; and The Lower Nile. Columbia
EC-38163 (LP, OP).

Reactionism triumphant is the key to pianist **Bobby Enriquez** (1944–   ), who, like Tatum, summarizes the whole
history of jazz piano in his playing. But while Tatum could
only summarize the playing of Morton, Johnson, Hines, and
Pine Top and only foreshadow the styles of Powell, Monk,
and Evans, Enriquez summarizes all these and more. There
are traces of funk, Erroll Garner's pixielike humor, Oscar
Peterson's sophistication, and even Tania Maria's Latin fire,
all wrapped up in the blinding speed of Tatum and a sense

of cohesion and direction in his improvisations, the likes of which haven't been heard in years.

Part of the key to Enriquez's pianistic personality may be seen in the large number of Charlie Parker compositions he plays. Like Powell, he tries to be a keyboard extension of a bop horn; unlike Powell (or even Tatum, for that matter), he aims not for a pretty sound but for a gusty, almost violent attack that has earned him the nickname "Wildman." But make no mistake, Enriquez is neither mad nor wild; in fact, as the second of the two following LPs shows, he is an even finer accompanist than Tatum, allowing altoist Richie Cole some breathing room instead of continually improvising behind him:

Prodigious Piano/Recado; Masquerade; The Shadow of Your Smile; Billie's Bounce; Here's That Rainy Day; Cherokee; Señor Blues; and Bossa Philadelphia. GNP Crescendo GNPS-2151 (LP).

The Wildman Meets the Madman (with Richie Cole)/Groovin' High; Once in a While; Yardbird Suite; Wild Man Blues; Green Dolphin Street; Serenata; Blue Hawaii; and Um Um. GNP Crescendo GNPS-2148 (LP).

The third great reactionary of our time is trumpeter **Wynton Marsalis** (1961–). Like Brubeck, he has received his share of media hype as the greatest genius/creator/improvisor to walk the face of the earth, praise that the young man has struggled to live up to. What Marsalis has actually done is to reestablish a pure, round tone to trumpet playing and to revive the more creative bop-cool school that was in flower the year he was born. Following a stint in Art Blakey's Jazz Messengers, he toured in late 1981 and early 1982 with the revived V.S.O.P. Quintet, then formed a group of his own, including his brother Branford on tenor and soprano sax, Ken Kirkland on piano, Phil Bowler on bass, and Jeffrey Watts on drums. Wynton Marsalis still has plenty of room to grow; but at least, as the following album shows, he has the right basic material:

> *Think of One*/Knozz-Moe-King; My Ideal; What Is Happening Here (Now)?; Fuchsia; The Bell Ringer; Think of One; Later; and Melancholia. CBS FC/CK/FCT-38641 (LP/CD/Cs).

As can be heard in the performances here, Wynton Marsalis takes a serious, cerebral approach to music. Some, in fact, would argue that he is *too* serious, that in his conscious effort to measure up to the giants of the past, his music is a little too self-conscious and shows too much effort. This attitude, however, seems not to bother either pianist Kirkland or Branford Marsalis, who appear to be more *creative* jazz musicians than Wynton. The success (if any) of the various Marsalis groups seems always to center around their contributions; when they are not present, Wynton's playing tends to be sterile and lacking focus.

Branford's own recording sessions emphasize both the similarities and the differences of the brothers to an amazing degree. Like Wynton, Branford's sax playing conjures up memories of former greats while exploring new avenues of improvisation; unlike Wynton, Branford manages to convey the emotional as well as the musical personality of his mentors. In the following album, for instance, he pays tribute to Ornette Coleman, Ben Webster, and Wayne Shorter with stunning accuracy, yet retains an individuality of expression that often eludes his more famous younger brother:

> *Random Abstract*/Yes and No; Crescent City; Broadway Fools; LonJellis; I Thought About You; Lonely Woman; Steep's Theme; Yesterdays; and Crepuscle With Nellie. CBS CK/OCT-44055 (CD/Cs).

Alternating with Kirkland in the Marsalis group was blind pianist **Marcus Roberts** (1963–   ), another reactionary and one of the most creative we have with us today. Roberts's style is deeply rooted in the blues, peppered with bop rhythms, and incorporates several elements of both Duke Ellington and Thelonious Monk. Roberts almost stands alone today as the supreme colorist of jazz; though his arrangements are not as compound-complex as those of Mingus, they also do not restrict the improvising soloist quite as much. In this respect he is not as interesting an orchestrator, yet his musical creations are profound and moving—more so, perhaps, than that of any other active pianist. As the opening track on the following album demonstrates, Roberts is not averse to adopting Eastern sounds to his explorations of the blues:

> *Deep in the Shed*/Nebuchadnezzar; Spiritual Awakening; The Governor; Deep in the Shed; Mysterious Interlude; and E. Dankworth. RCA/Novus 3078-1/2/4-N (LP/CD/Cs).

One of the most remarkable performers to make an impact during the 1980s and one of the greatest jazz singers is **Sheila Jordan** (1928–   ). A musical stepchild of the bop era, Jordan formed her roots in the music of Parker and Billie Holiday, though she continued to grow and expand with the vocabulary of the cool and postcool generations. She made her debut album for Blue Note in 1963; yet, though *down beat* hailed her as "one of the discoveries of 1963," the LP was soon deleted from the catalog. In 1977 she waxed an album in Norway with no more accompaniment than the solo acoustic bass of **Arild Andersen** (1946–   ); it was not released in this country until 1985. Despite its strangeness, it has become a strong underground seller:

> *Sheila*/Song of Joy; Hold Out Your Hand; Lush Life; The Saga of Harrison Crabfeathers; Green Dolphin Street; What Are You Doing the Rest of Your Life?; It Never Entered My Mind; Better Than Anything; Don't Explain; The Lady; and Please Don't Talk About Me When I'm Gone. SteepleChase SCS-1081/SCCD-31081/SCC-1081 (LP/CD/Cs).

Jordan's voice is a high mezzo-soprano. The tone is light but the timbre dark, and she utilizes an extraordinary range of vocal effects to bend and color the voice as no other jazz singer has done. At times her sound is fragile and wistful, at others thick and filled with pain. Her style is unusual, pulling and pushing the tone as she weaves absolute magic in this collection of standards and oddities. Listening to the album in toto, one is astonished at how strongly the songs are bound together; this is jazz's greatest song cycle, a musical auto-biography as compelling in its own way as Franz Schubert's *Winterreise*.

The year 1983 saw the rise of bass guitarist **Jamaaladeen Tacuma** (1957–), né Rudy McDaniel, who moved from R&B to progressive jazz via Ornette Coleman's group. In addition to being a spectacular bassist, technically equaling acoustic players such as Mingus, Gomez, and Anderson, Tacuma possessed a highly focused and creative musical mind that seemed to congeal complex and disparate elements effortlessly. He took Coleman's concept of "harmolodics" to new heights, and showed a flair for truly creative classical composition. The following album, certainly his best, sums up the full range of his talent:

> *Renaissance Man*/Renaissance Man; Flash Back; Let's Have a Good Time; The Next Stop; Dancing in Your Head; There He Stood; Battle of Images; and Sparkle. Gramavision R21K/R41E-79438 (CD/Cs).

On the above album, the first four tracks feature his regular performing group, Jamaal. "Dancing in Your Head" is a remake of a 1977 Coleman composition, with Ornette guesting on alto sax. "There He Stood," a poem set to music, honors Paul Robeson; "Sparkle" is an up-tempo jam. But "Battle of Images" is unique, being a modern classical composition for string quartet, electric bass, and percussion that really works in both the classical and jazz contexts. Unfortunately, the Ebony String Quartet is sadly out of tune.

In the years since 1985, the trend has been toward a new

type of "fusion," this time utilizing the oversynthesized sound of modern rock. Very little of it is really jazz, and even less of it works, but in the pursuit of social idolatry and platinum albums we are inundated with discs by such third-rate talents as Spyro Gyra, Dave Valentin, Kazumi Watanabe, Kenny G., Peri, and the Rippingtons. An offshoot of this has been "New Age" music, a form of modern Muzak utilizing jazz techniques yet containing precious little jazz content. Among the worst of these performers have been pianist George Winston and the vocal/guitar duo Tuck and Patti.

Curiously, the album that led this trend was innovative, creative, and—despite some bizarre qualities—highly musical. This was a 1984 tribute to Thelonious Monk featuring rock *and* jazz musicians. Usually such "crossover" projects emerge as pretentious garbage, but producer Hal Willner showed unusual taste in judgment, selecting participants who already knew and admired Monk. The result was a blockbuster seller, for jazz:

> *That's the Way I Feel Now*/Thelonious; Four in One; Reflections; Blue Monk; Ask Me Now; Little Rootie Tootie; Brilliant Corners; Monk's Mood; Pannonica; Ba-Lue-Bolivar-Ba-Lues-Are; Shuffle Boil; Misterioso; 'Round Midnight; Evidence; Work; Functional; and Bemsha Swing. A&M SP/CD/CS-6600 (two LPs/one CD/one Cs).

The featured artists included such famous rock acts as Peter Frampton, Dr. John, NRBQ, and Todd Rundgren, in addition to renowned Monk interpreters such as saxist Steve Lacy and Gil Evans. Avant-garde groups Was (Not Was) and the Carla Bley Band are here, as is Sheila Jordan (in a supporting role). Yet it works—despite the fact that a number of albums conceived in the same vein, yet musically anemic, do not.

The resounding artistic and popular success in latter years of soprano saxist **Steve Lacy** (1934–) helps one understand just how profound Monk's influence was on all modern jazz. Lacy came into his own after playing with Monk in the late

1950s and early 1960s, to create music that ranges from profoundly disturbing to simply profound. Yet his style, despite the Monk influence, is eclectic. Before his stint with Monk he also worked with avant-garde guru Cecil Taylor, and as a result he sometimes combines both the best and worst aspects of such players as Dolphy, Coltrane, and Coleman in his own compositions and improvisations. In some of his own works—for instance, "Prelude and Anthem," in the following disc—he shows a marked tendency not to emulate the ordered form of Monk (as he does in "Number One") but to muck with the chaos of "free jazz" in a pretentious setting. This particular alliance is odd, though it shows that Lacy is a musician willing to take risks. Nevertheless, it marks (for me) a weak point in an otherwise superb exploration of modern sounds, including a "New Age" feel in "J.J.'s Jam":

Anthem/Number One; Prayer; J.J.'s Jam; Prelude and Anthem; The Mantle; and The Rent. Novus 3079-2-N.

One of the few jazz musicians to emerge from the rock-R&B scene and produce music of lasting value is tenor saxist **Michael Brecker** (1949–   ). Brecker is so great and powerful a player that many feel he has picked up where Coltrane left off—before Coltrane's final two years of craziness, of course. Exploring various corners of the hard-bop repertoire, both on tenor and an eight-octave electronic wind instrument called the Akai EWI, Brecker is joined on his albums by such established jazz stars as pianist Herbie Hancock, bassist Charlie Haden, and drummer Jackie DeJohnette, who aid greatly in the creative process. Brecker has an astounding technique and power to burn, yet none of his phrases gives the impression of useless rhetoric. As the following album shows, he tries to produce jazz with integrity—something that seems to have disappeared in this high-tech, soulless age:

Don't Try This at Home/Itsbynne Reel; Scriabin; Suspone; Everything Happens When You're Gone; Chime This; Don't Try This at Home; and Talking to Myself. MCA/ Impulse! MCA/MCAD-42229 (LP/CD).

The last bastion of jazz creativity today seems to be in those few groups, comprised of virtuoso musicians, who stay together and explore the music's depths. I cite three in particular: the World Saxophone Quartet, the Turtle Island String Quartet, and the Dirty Dozen Brass Band. Their styles are very different from one another, yet together they create some truly amazing music.

The oldest of these is the **World Saxophone Quartet,** formed in the late 1970s. The component members of the band—**David Murray** (1955–   ), **Oliver Lake** (1942–   ), **Julius Hemphill** (1951–   ), and **Hamiet Bluiett** (1940–   )— are all innovative players, encompassing a wide range on their instruments (Bluiett, in fact, can extend the baritone sax into the *soprano* range!) and including flute and bass clarinet in addition to the usual array of saxes. Their music is incredibly dense, both rhythmically and harmonically; they often use techniques (compositionally and in playing their instruments) borrowed from modern classical music. They pursue the type of organized chaos that characterized the playing of Eric Dolphy. Though the component members of the band (especially Murray) emulate Dolphy's lack of form and structure on their solo albums, their playing together has an amazing consistency and sense of purpose:

Steppin' with the W.S.Q./Steppin'; Ra-Ta-Ta; Dream Schemes; P.O. in Cairo; R&B; and Hearts. Black Saint BSR-0046/120-046-2 (LP/CD).

As can be heard, their creativity and rhythmic sense (working a cappella) is phenomenal. Like Mingus, they are wise enough to change the underlying harmonic structure when they explore multitonal or atonal improvisations; the rapidity with which the others can follow each individual's improvisation is uncanny, revealing highly disciplined musical minds. Conversely, like modern classical music, a little bit goes a long way. They are best taken in small doses, when wide awake and willing to come to the music.

Something of the sort may be said about the **Turtle Island String Quartet**, a group co-founded by violinists Darol Anger and David Balakrishnan. Their music is highly eclectic, taking elements of American Indian, bluegrass, East Indian, and classical music under their wing; yet the main thrust of their style is to produce a fantastically high-quality bop. Considering that these are acoustic instruments of the type normally associated with the Budapest String Quartet, one is constantly amazed at their versatility, as in the following album:

> *Turtle Island String Quartet*/Stolen Moments; Night in Tunisia; Milestones; Tempus Fugit; String Quartet No. 1; Balapadem; and Decline of an American String Quartet. Windham Hill WH/WD-0110 (LP/CD).

In this debut album, Balakrishnan's work as composer and arranger is dominant, possibly because he is the most adroit at adapting this offbeat and uncharted material for string quartet. In the improvisations, however, Anger, violist Irene Sazer, and cellist Mark Summer take a backseat to no one. Their technique is astonishing, utilizing pizzicato on the cello more reminiscent of Jimmy Blanton than of Emanuel Feuermann; employing bow-scraping that simulates the sound of brushes on drums and cymbals; and, in general, revolutionizing their instruments within the classical-jazz framework. One must listen several times to get past the *how* of their playing to get to the *what*; but the effort proves worthwhile. Turtle Island is more than just the first string group of its kind to swing; they are simultaneously creative and entertaining in a way that few modern jazz groups are.

So, too, is the **Dirty Dozen Brass Band**, a latter-day representation of New Orleans style that incorporates all of the city's musical innovations, from the brass-band days to the present. It boasts a superb "front line" of trumpeter Gregory Davis, trombonist Charles Joseph, tenor saxist Kevin Harris, baritone saxist Roger Lewis, and drummer Jenell Marshall. It utilizes this traditional instrumentation in an advanced, beboppish mode, and its rhythms are a combination of hard-bop, R&B, and Professor Longhair's calypso beat. For a final dash of zest, it performs everything in its repertoire with a vigor that makes it almost impossible for the listener not to get up and dance.

Unlike many modern outfits, Dirty Dozen's main purpose is to have its audiences *enjoy* its playing. Even in concert halls, trumpeter Davis can be heard exhorting the audience to get up and move around—the complete antithesis to the majority of modern jazz, which is intended for listening. As the following album clearly demonstrates, this feeling of enjoyment is never far away, even in the band's most complex arrangements:

> *Voodoo*/It's All Over Now; Don't Drive Drunk; Gemini Rising; Oop Pop a Dah; Moose the Mooche; Voodoo; Black Drawers/Blue Piccolo; and Santa Cruz. CBS CJ/CK/FCT-45042 (LP/CD/Cs).

As can be heard in the above selections, Dirty Dozen has incorporated the island backbeats (via Trinidad and Jamaica) in a way that few New Orleans jazz musicians have done. The bold, adventurous trombone playing of Charles Joseph is especially enticing with its high-note excursions, but every member of this fabulous group has something wonderful to offer. They have, in effect, reinvented the riff, and revitalized the Crescent City style in a way that Wynton Marsalis can only dream about.

Curiously, as the 1990s begin to emerge, the two musicians who still exert as strong an influence today as they did when they were alive are pianist Bill Evans and bassist Charlie Mingus. The vast majority of our piano trios are not so much in the shadow of Nat "King" Cole or Art Tatum as they are in the work that Evans pioneered so successfully in the early 1960s; and just about every other modern stream, avant-garde or otherwise, owes a huge debt to the work of Mingus. One player who started his career in Mingus's last band was trumpeter **Jack Walrath** (1947–   ), who has emerged in latter years as a composer and organizer astonishingly on a par with the master. Like Mingus, Walrath believes in chance improvisations, as well as in organizing one's forces only to the point where the individual contributions do not get out of hand musically. Only a portion of his music is as soul-wrenching as Mingus's, but he gets the point across fairly well, as the following album shows:

> *Neohippus*/Village of the Darned; Watch Your Head; Fright Night; Annie Lee; England; Beer!; Future Reference; and The Smell of the Blues. Blue Note B11H/CDP/ B41H-91101 (LP/CD/Cs).

Probably the most astonishing jazz album of all time, as a voice beyond the grave beckoning us in new directions we have not yet tried while combining these with roads well traveled, is Charles Mingus's *Epitaph*. This sprawling, two-hour work, pieced together by musicologist Gunther Schuller (who also conducts), runs the full gamut of musical experience from early jazz, blues, and church music through the most sophisticated minds of all time, such as Monk, Strayhorn, and Ellington; the whole is suffused with the spirit and musical imagination of one of jazz's great geniuses; and the whole, as presented on record, is an astonishing blend of seriousness, whimsy, black humor, boisterous laughter, emotional release, and the chill of death. No one album sums up the entire history of jazz—past, present, *and* future—nearly as well as this half-breed work of Mingus's. And if, after the first fifteen minutes or so, it doesn't hold together as a "jazz symphony" as well as it should, this is more than compensated for by the boldness and emotional pull of the music:

> *Epitaph*/Main Score Part 1; Percussion Discussion; Main Score Part 2; Started Melody; Better Git It in Your Soul;

The Soul; Moods in Mambo; Self Portrait/Chill of Death; O.P. (Oscar Pettiford); Please Don't Come Back From the Moon; Monk, Bunk & Vice Versa (Osmotin); Peggy's Blue Skylight; Wolverine Blues; The Children's Hour of Dream; Ballad; Freedom; Interlude (The Underdog Rising); Noon Night; and Main Score Reprise. Columbia/CBS C2K/C2T-45428 (two CDs/Cs).

Describing this music in less than a thousand words is impossible; it alternates between swinging big-band jazz such as "Main Score" and "Moods in Mambo," lovely jazz ballads such as "Started Melody," stark modern-classical pieces such as "Chill of Death" and "The Childen's Hour of Dream," and wild, imaginative flights of fancy such as "Monk, Bunk & Vice Versa" and his multilayered arrangement of Jelly Roll Morton's "Wolverine Blues." In other words, this is Charles Mingus, in every facet of his personality. The assemblage of musicians reads like a Who's Who, including trumpeters Randy Brecker, Wynton Marsalis, Lew Soloff, Jack Walrath, Joe Wilder, and Snooky Young; trombonists Eddie Bert, Urbie Green, and Britt Woodman; saxists John Handy, Bobby Watson, and George Adams; tuba player Don Butterfield; and pianist Sir Roland Hanna.

Thus we stand, in the 1990s, on the threshold of a new era. Where will jazz go from here? Will it evolve, via Turtle Island, Tacuma, Lacy, Dirty Dozen, and the World Saxophone Quartet, into something new and enticing, or will it retract? Will regurgitated synthesizers rule the domain, or rust into the scrap heaps they so richly deserve? Will reactionaries such as Tania Maria, Enriquez, and Wynton Marsalis grow and change, or stagnate in their present styles? No one can answer those questions; by rights, no one should. If jazz is to remain a music of "surprise," then none should try to second-guess the musicians. They and they alone possess the key to the future, if there is one. In the meantime, the past has been a gas.

Epilogue

In compiling this book, and in choosing whom to include and whom to omit, personal tastes played but a small part; I decided in ninety-nine cases out of a hundred to go with established critical opinion as to who were the most influential and creative musicians of any given era. This, of course, does not mean that I disliked all of the musicians I felt impelled to include—far from it, I am deeply in love with a great many of them—but it does explain why I included certain musicians to whom I gave an ambivalent or negative assessment. They may not have been my personal favorites, but they *were* important.

Conversely, this is the reason I left out peripheral jazz artists including Diane Schuur and Harry Connick, Jr., as well as such eclectic figures (whom I do like) as Harry "The Hipster" Gibson, Ray Charles, and the early Pointer Sisters. More painful, to me, was the decision to eliminate such one-of-a-kind artists as jazz tap dancer Baby Laurence and "word jazz" poet Ken Nordine; they were *so* unusual that they had virtually no followers. No one could do what they did.

Of course, this should lead readers to the point where they can make up their own minds regarding certain figures in jazz's rich history. For my own part, I often enjoy the offbeat creativity of Lacy, Tacuma, and the World Saxophone Quartet, but when I want to hear "home cookin' " I turn to the recordings of Morton, Beiderbecke, Ellington, Armstrong, Eldridge, Teagarden, Kirby, Bechet, Gillespie, Parker, Nat Cole, Hampton, Monk, Mulligan, Brubeck, and Mingus. Wild abandon and creativity are all very well and good, but I feel more assured when I hear musicians who knew what they wanted and how to get it, though of course even in the past not all jazz musicians were of equal merit. There has been an astounding amount of jazz played through the decades, today more so (it seems) than ever. Developing a keen ear and some sort of personal guidelines will prevent you from being suckered into the general consensus that all jazz has merit. It certainly is not created equal, any more than classical music was.

Basic Jazz Terms

Several jazz terms are used in the text. Many of these are either explained, or self-explanatory; others, such as "jam session" and "gig," have become so much a part of our vernacular that they need no explanation. On the other hand, a few terms may still be confusing to the lay reader, and/or insufficiently explained in the text. For that reason I have included the following short list of definitions:

Barrelhouse   An early form of piano playing that emphasized rhythmic drive over melodic improvisation; developed in New Orleans and moved to Chicago. Most barrelhouse playing was influenced by the blues and in turn was one influence on boogie. Today it is largely extinct, except for some older practitioners of the New Orleans and/or Chicago style.

Bombs   Heavily accented beats on the bass drum, thrown into the rhythmic pattern at odd intervals—for instance, on the second beat (out of four) instead of on the first or third. This was a specific development of the bebop style and was later superseded by a slicker, more polyrhythmic style of drumming that influenced and supported the "modern" style that followed bop.

Break   One- or two-bar interludes, often (though not always) at the end of a chorus (*see* chorus), where the soloist improvises a connecting phrase while the other instruments temporarily "drop out." In early jazz, breaks were primarily rhythmic, but Louis Armstrong developed a style in which the rhythmic pulse was matched by alternative melodic ideas, while Jelly Roll Morton used breaks to supply a "fill-in" by differing instruments to provide extra sound coloring. Morton described the break as "a musical surprise," a definition that still holds today.

Chase　An improvised chorus (or series of choruses) played by two instruments: sometimes one brass and one reed instrument, but possibly by two "competing" instruments in the same family. These then alternate phrases in eight-, four-, or two-bar segments, much like the "dueling banjos" of folk music; the interest heightens when a chase chorus is completely improvised, the musicians using the last note (or notes) of the previous phrase as a takeoff for their own contribution. This style was first developed into high art in the 1920s by C-melody saxist Frank Trumbauer and cornetist Bix Beiderbecke. Other famous "chase chorus" teams have been tenor saxists Wardell Gray and Dexter Gordon as well as baritone saxist Gerry Mulligan and trumpeter Chet Baker.

Chorus　Generally refers to a complete thirty-two-bar statement within the structure of popular song forms adapted to jazz, and/ or a twelve- or twenty-four-bar statement in the blues. Half choruses are obvious reductions of these.

Coda　One of the few terms borrowed from classical music; as defined in *Baker's Dictionary of Musical Terms*, a "tail," hence a passage ending a movement. Like the break, this is often played *sans* rhythm section and can be either by a solo instrument or by the full group.

Comp　A rhythmic underpinning to a played or sung chorus and meant as an abbreviation for "accompaniment." It is generally a series of chords played either on or off the principal beat. Simple as it sounds, comping is an art unto itself; singers who played piano often tried it themselves, with mixed results. The most successful and creative self-comping was the style perfected in the 1940s by Nat "King" Cole.

Dixieland A pseudo-jazz "style" using the traditional New Orleans or Chicago front line of cornet (or trumpet), clarinet, trombone, and optional saxophone in a slick, commercial manner. This style was developed and honed to perfection in New York during the early 1930s by the Dorsey Brothers' Orchestra, though it is generally associated today with smaller groups of one instrument each. This style is marked by a very simple rhythmic beat, 2/4, which is closer to ragtime than to true jazz. Ironically, both the name and the style originated with a true jazz group, The Original Dixieland Jazz Band, in the late 1910s; as an unfortunate compromise to the short length of the 78-rpm record, they often omitted solos in favor of ensemble choruses—yet another artistic casualty of earlier restrictions on jazz.

Funk or funky A word originally applied to solos (and, later, ensembles) that had a bluesy, almost "dirty" intonation; certain notes, played with a raspy tone, were said to be "funky," implying that there was some spit left in the horn. In latter years the definition has shifted somewhat, applying to a large assortment of popular music played and sung by blacks, including rap music, much of which is actually a slick adaptation of the real thing. As a result, the term has become meaningless, but is used in the context of this book to denote the real thing.

Groove A descriptive term that generally refers to a solidly swinging feeling that permeates a chorus or an entire performance. Musicians often talk of being "in the groove" or "in a good groove" as a way of expressing the ultimate jazz feeling. This term was popularized by bop trumpeter Dizzy Gillespie in his classic composition "Groovin' High."

Jump Used interactively as an adjective or a verb. In the former, "jump music" was used to describe the boisterous, often simpler music of small-group jazz; in the latter, used as an alternative to "swing."

Mainstream A term briefly used at one time by critic Stanley Dance to identify the kind of jazz increasingly excluded by the warring factions of the New Orleans and bebop idioms (late 1940s to late 1950s), both of which were then enjoying exaggerated publicity. In recent years, it has come to refer almost exclusively to the swing style.

Mode Another term borrowed from classical music, it refers to the scale used as the basis for a composition and its component improvisations. The two most common "modes" are major or minor; the bop "mode" generally substituted a flatted fifth for an open one in both cases. Since the 1950s the term has also been used to describe more offbeat scales, such as the whole tone; Eastern modes that use different sharped or flatted notes; chromatic scales; and the twelve-tone row, in which the notes of the chromatic scale (encompassing twelve half tones from top to bottom of an octave, or—more simply—every black and white key on the piano between two notes an octave apart) are used in a random but prealigned order.

New Orleans style A worked-out system of collective improvisation in which the trumpet (or cornet) plays the lead, the clarinet plays free counterpoint improvisation, and the trombone works out the lower harmonies. Variations include a second trumpet and/or extra reed player, as in King Oliver's Creole Jazz Band or the New Orleans Rhythm Kings. Sometimes the clarinet and trumpet (cornet) exchange roles in the course of a chorus, and occasionally one or more of these instruments steps forward for a solo turn. Not to be confused with Dixieland, which is a simplification and bastardization of what is, in reality, a complex and difficult yet beautiful style.

Riff A repeated rhythmic-melodic figure used as a unit and reiterated to produce a full chorus and/or an ensemble break (*see* break). This was used as far back as the New Orleans days but was developed into a recurring style by the Kansas City swing bands of the 1930s, particularly that of Count Basie.

Slap-tongue An obsolete technique of playing reed instruments, mostly the saxophone but sometimes the clarinet as well, and that came from vaudeville music; it consisted of placing the tongue on and off the reed while playing separate notes, which gave the music a "slapping" sound. It was sometimes used by old New Orleans players around the turn of the century, though the best of them (Johnny Dodds, Sidney Bechet, and Jimmy Noone) dropped it very early in their careers. Saxophonists, on the other hand, persisted on carrying it into the New York style of the 1920s; even such early masters as Coleman Hawkins and Frank Trumbauer spent years escaping its influence.

Stomp An early jazz term that described a slightly faster than middle-tempo piece, with heavy emphasis on the first and third beats. By the late 1920s it was also used to describe any up-tempo piece with a heavy rhythmic push; thus, like "funk," it is a term that often has more than one meaning. It was also used colloquially by jazz musicians as a verb indicating a lively "kickoff" to a tune, as in the phrase "stomp off."

Third stream A term coined in the 1950s by jazz musicologist Gunther Schuller to describe music that is neither purely jazz nor purely classical, but a hybrid. This type of music was pioneered by Duke Ellington, though its first truly successful exponent was pianist/arranger Claude Thornhill in the early 1940s. Some of the music of George Russell, Charles Mingus, and even Darius Milhaud can also be classified as third stream.

Tone cluster A term that refers to a group of adjacent keyboard notes played simultaneously by fingers, fist, or forearm. Its sound, to the naked ear, resembles that of a cat walking on a piano and hitting two or three keys at once.

Vamp A rhythmic introduction to a chorus or a complete tune, generally played on the piano but sometimes by lower brass instruments; similar, but not identical, to a comp (*see* comp), it often utilizes a short riff form (*see* riff), which makes it slightly melodic and/or harmonic in addition to its rhythmic quality.

Voicing A term taken from classical music but given an entirely different meaning. In classical terms, voicing refers to the registration of organs, which gives the instrument different sounds or "voices"; in jazz terms, voicing is the blending or mixing of different instruments, with or without mutes, to produce unique sounds that can only come from that particular blend (and sometimes only from those particular performers). The pioneers of jazz voicing were Jelly Roll Morton (old style) and Duke Ellington (New York style), though it has become a recurrent, almost trademark feature of modern jazz. Its most famous exponents (after the swing era) have been Thelonious Monk, Charles Mingus, and Gil Evans.

A Basic Jazz Library:
Sixty Albums

Roughly 140 albums are recommended in this book, to give an aural guide to the music. Considering that some discs are out of print or hard to find, however, plus the fact that buying all of them may strain one's finances, they can be reduced to less than half. Of course, making such a selection is subjective, and assumes an interest in one field or another that the listener/reader may not have; but as a concise overview of all eras under consideration, these are the best recommendations I can make (following the chronology of the book):

Jazz, Vol. 3: New Orleans. Folkways FJ-2803 (LP).
Jazz, Vol. 11: Addenda. Folkways FJ-2811 (LP).
New Orleans Rhythm Kings. Milestone M-47020 (CD).
Bix Beiderbecke. BBC Records REB/CD/ZCF-601 (LP/CD/Cs).
At the Jazz Band Ball/Condon, Spanier, Freeman. RCA 6752-2-RB (CD).
Louis Armstrong. BBC Records REB/CD/ZCF-597 (LP/CD/Cs).
Piano in Style, 1926–1930. MCA/MCAC-1332 (LP/Cs).
Bessie Smith: The Collection. CBS CJ/CK/CJT-44441 (LP/CD/Cs).
Jelly Roll Morton: The Pearls. RCA Bluebird 6588-1/2/4-RB (LP/CD/Cs).
Building an American Orchestra/Fletcher Henderson. Smithsonian Collection P2-13710 (2 LPs)

Gotta Right to Sing the Blues/Jack Teagarden. ASV AJA/CDAJA-5059 (LP/CD).

Rhythm of the Day/Red Nichols. ASV/Living Era AJA/CDAJA-5025 (LP/CD).

Early Ellington/Duke Ellington. RCA Bluebird 6852-1/2/4-RB (LP/CD/Cs).

Best of the Big Bands: Glen Gray. CBS CK/CJT-45345 (CD/Cs).

The Legendary Sidney Bechet. RCA Bluebird 6590-1/2/4-RB (LP/CD/Cs).

Everybody Loves My Baby/The Boswell Sisters. Pro Arte CDD-550 (CD).

The Definitive Fats Waller, Vol. 1. Stash ST-CD-528 (CD).

Django '35–'39/Django Reinhardt. GNP Crescendo GNP-9019 (LP).

Piano Starts Here/Art Tatum. Columbia PG/PCT-32121 (LP/Cs).

Tatum-Carter-Bellson. Pablo 2310/52310-732/733, 2405-424-2 (2 LP/Cs/1 CD).

The Benny Goodman Story. MCA 4055-2/MCAD-4055 (2 LPs/1 CD).

The Blanton-Webster Band/Duke Ellington. RCA 5659-1/2/4-RB (4 LPs, 3 CD/Cs).

One O'Clock Jump/Count Basie. MCA/MCAD/MCAC-42324 (LP/CD/Cs).

The Billie Holiday Story, Vol. 1. Columbia PG-32121 (2 LPs).

Earl Hines: Piano Man. RCA Bluebird 6750-1/2/4-RB (LP/CD/Cs).

Red Norvo Featuring Mildred Bailey. Portrait Masters RK-44118 (CD).

Louis Armstrong 4: Swing That Music (OP). MCA/MCAC-1312 (LP/Cs).

Uptown/Roy Eldridge, Anita O'Day, Gene Krupa. CBS CK/CJT-45448 (CD/Cs).

Body and Soul/Coleman Hawkins. RCA 5658-1/4-RB, 5717-2-RB (2 LPs/Cs, 1 CD).

Biggest Band in the Land/John Kirby Sextet. Smithsonian P2-14584 (2 LPs).

Jumpin' At Capitol/Nat "King" Cole Trio. Rhino R21S/R41H-71009 (CD/Cs).

The Thundering Herds/Woody Herman. CBS CJ/CK/CJT-44108 (LP/CD/Cs).

Boyd Raeburn: Rare Broadcast Performances. Echo Jazz EJCD-13 (CD).

The Legendary Dial Masters, Vol. 1/Charlie Parker. Stash ST-CD-23 (CD).

Dizziest/Dizzy Gillespie. RCA Bluebird 5785-1-RB (2 LPs).

The Complete Genius/Thelonious Monk. Blue Note LWB-00579/ CDP-81510-11 (2 LPs/CDs).

A Charlie Ventura Concert. MCA/MCAC/MCAD-42330 (LP/Cs/CD).

Complete Birth of the Cool/Miles Davis. Capitol N-16168/CDP-92862 (LP/CD).

The Best of the Gerry Mulligan Quartet with Chet Baker. Pacific Jazz CDP7-95481 (CD).

At Basin Street/Clifford Brown. EmArcy EXPR-1033/814 648-2 (LP/ CD).

Sarah Vaughan. EmArcy EXPR-1009/814 641-2 (LP/CD).

Compact Jazz: Ella Fitzgerald. Verve 831 367-2/4 (CD/Cs).

Django/The Modern Jazz Quartet. Prestige OJC/OJCCD-057 (LP/ CD).

Time Out/The Dave Brubeck Quartet. CBS CJ/CK/CJT-40648 (LP/ CD/Cs).

Mingus Ah Um/Charles Mingus. CBS CJ/CK/CJT-40648 (LP/ CD/Cs).

Mingus at Antibes/Charles Mingus. Atlantic 90532-1/2/4 (LP/CD/Cs).

Everybody's Boppin'/Lambert, Hendricks, and Ross. CBS CJ/CK/CJT-45020 (LP/CD/Cs).

Kind of Blue/Miles Davis. CBS CJ/CK/CJT-40579 (LP/CD/Cs).

Sunday at the Village Vanguard/Bill Evans. Riverside OJC/OJCCD-140 (LP/CD).

Coltrane Jazz/John Coltrane. Atlantic SD-1354/1354-2 (LP/CD).

Return to Forever/Chick Corea. ECM 811978-1/2/4 (LP/CD/Cs).

The Toshiko Akiyoshi–Lew Tabackin Big Band. RCA/Novus 3106-2-N (CD).

V.S.O.P.—The Quintet. Columbia C2-34976 (2 LPs).

Elaborations/Arthur Blythe. Columbia EC-38163 (LP, OP).

Prodigious Piano/Bobby Enriquez. GNP Crescendo GNPS-2151 (LP).

Deep in the Shed/Marcus Roberts. RCA/Novus 3078-1/2/4-N (LP/CD/ Cs).

Sheila/Sheila Jordan. SteepleChase SCS-1081/SCCD-31081 (LP/CD).

Steppin' with the World Saxophone Quartet. Black Saint BSR-0046/120-046-2 (LP/CD).

Turtle Island String Quartet. Windham Hill WH/WD/WT-0110 (LP/ CD/Cs).

Voodoo/Dirty Dozen Brass Band. CBS CJ/CK/FCT-45042 (LP/CD/Cs).

Regarding some of the smaller or offbeat labels recommended, here are some addresses and/or telephone numbers for your convenience:

BBC Records: Distributed by Allegro Imports, 3434 N. Milwaukie Ave., Portland, OR 97202; tel. (800) 288-2007.

Folkways: Rounder Records, 1 Camp St., Cambridge, MA 02140; tel. (617) 354-0700.

IAJRS/Stash/Tax: Stash Records, 611 Broadway, Suite 725, New York, NY 10012; tel. (800) 666-5277.

Living Era/ASV: Distributed by Harmonia Mundi USA, 3364 S. Robertson Blvd., Los Angeles, CA 90034; tel. (213) 559-0802.

Rhino Records: Rhino Records, Inc., Department C-11d, 2225 Colorado Ave., Santa Monica, CA 90404-3555; tel. (800) 432-0020.

Savoy: Muse Records, 160 W. 71st St., New York, NY 10023; tel. (212) 873-2020.

SteepleChase: 3943 W. Lawrence Ave., Chicago, IL 60625; tel. (312) 463-6147.

Vocalion: Distributed by MCA, 70 Universal City Plaza, Universal City, CA 91608; tel. (818) 777-4000.

Jazz on Compact Discs

In the past few years, compact discs have come out of nowhere to supplement and, one thinks, eventually supplant the LP record. Digital remastering often (but not always) clarifies textures in older monophonic and early stereo recordings, and the CD has the advantages of longer life and no surface noise.

Insofar as historic jazz reissues are concerned, however, the CD market is hardly overripe with a bumper crop. MCA hasn't issued even one of their French-produced LP series on CD; CBS seems to think that none of Ellington's 1932–1937 output is worth hearing on the new medium, and refuses to give us more than sixteen titles per album (until recently—they seem to be reversing this trend); and RCA, though making some impressive inroads with earlier material, seems to prefer one-disc "collections" rather than multidisc sets (the Ellington 1940–1942 band being a rare exception). Nevertheless, there *are* some CDs of note available other than those mentioned in the text. The best of these are, therefore, listed for further perusal by the reader.

Sidney Bechet: The Olympia Concert/While in no way supplanting the superb RCA recordings, this CD contains unusually forward and vivid 1955 performances at the Olympia in Paris, with the 1920s-styled big bands of André Reweliotty and Claude Luter: Blues in the Air; Wild Man Blues; Wild Cat Rag; I Don't Know Where I'm Going; Viper Mad; Southern Sunset; Les Oignons; Halle Hallelujah; Dans les Rues d'Antibes; Panama Rag; When the Saints Go Marchin' In; and Royal Garden Blues. French Vogue 600023 (Rounder Records, 1 Camp Street, Cambridge, MA 02140; tel. 617-354-0700).

Sidney Bechet: The Victor Sessions—Master Takes, 1932–43/This recent reissue of Bechet's complete RCA output is highly recommended for his fans; after all, Bechet is one of those rare jazzmen you really can't get enough of. RCA Bluebird 2402-2-RB (three CDs).

Bix 'n' Bing/Recordings by Beiderbecke and Crosby with Paul Whiteman's Orchestra, 1927–1929: Mary; Changes; There Ain't No Sweet Man; Louisiana; From Monday On; Lovable; My Pet; You Took Advantage of Me; Do I Hear You Saying "I Love You"?; High Water; Sunshine; 'Tain't So, Honey; That's My Weakness Now; Because My Baby Don't Mean Maybe Now; I'm in the Seventh Heaven; Reaching for Someone; Oh, Miss Hannah; Your Mother and Mine; and Waiting at the End of the Road. Living Era/ASV CDAJA-5005 (British).

Bix Lives!/This Victor CD repeats the first eight titles on the above, but the sonics are vastly superior and the album contains more titles from the Goldkette-Whiteman period, plus two 1930 cuts by Bix's studio band: Clementine; Proud of a Baby Like You; Lonely Melody; Smile; San; Back in Your Own Backyard; The Love Nest; Dardanella; Sugar; Coquette; When (two tks.); Forget-Me-Not; Deep Down South; and I'll Be a Friend "With Pleasure." RCA Bluebird 6845-2-RB.

The OKeh Ellington/This fairly recent two-CD compilation contains many of the early recordings formerly available on the out-of-print *Ellington Era* LPs (see Chapters 2 and 4), such as: East St. Louis Toodle-Oo; Hop Head; Black and Tan Fantasy; Jubilee Stomp; The Mooche; Hot and Bothered; Blues With a Feelin'; Lazy Duke; Old Man Blues; Mood Indigo; and Rockin' in Rhythm, in addition to such rarities as That Rhythm Man; Misty Mornin'; Freeze and Melt; Mississippi Moan; Snake Hip Dance; Syncopated Shuffle; Ragamuffin Romeo; Double Check Stomp; Big House Blues; and an acoustic version of Bugle Call Rag, among others. It should be noted, however, that it is NOT recommended over *The Ellington Era* because it omits the bulk of that set, which are the magnificent 1932–1939 Columbia, Brunswick, Master, and Vocalion sides that really set the Ellington style and contributed most significantly to his stature as the preeminent composer/arranger in big band jazz. CBS C2K-46177.

Dizzy Gillespie: With the oddness typical of commercial record labels, RCA has issued ten titles by the Gillespie big band, and four tracks by his 1946 sextet, on the album *The Bebop Revolution* (RCA Bluebird 2177-2-RB). This disc is not recommended as a substitute for the much better two-LP set *Dizziest* (see text), but it is a viable alternative for those who wish to have at least a few of the Gillespie big band's works in a more permanent form.

*The Quintessential Billie Holiday/*The first three volumes duplicate many of the studio discs in the recommended two-LP set. Vol. 1: Your Mother's Son-in-Law; Riffin' the Scotch; I Wished on the Moon; I'm Painting the Town Red; What a Little Moonlight Can Do; Miss Brown to You; A Sunbonnet Blue; What a Night, What a Moon, What a Girl; It's Too Hot for Words; 24 Hours a Day; Eeny Meeny Miney Mo; These 'n' That 'n' Those; Yankee Doodle Never Went to Town; If You Were Mine; You Let Me Down; Spreadin' Rhythm Around. CBS CK-40646. Vol. 2: Life Begins When You're in Love; These Foolish Things; I Cried for You; Reaching for the Moon; Guess Who; No Regrets; I Can't Pretend; Did I Remember?; Summertime; Billie's Blues; A Fine Romance; 1, 2, Button Your Shoe; Let's Call a Heart a Heart; Easy to Love; With Thee I Swing; The Way You Look Tonight. CBS CK-40790. Vol. 3: Who Loves You?; Pennies From Heaven; I Can't Give You Anything But Love; That's Life, I Guess; Please Keep Me in Your Dreams; One Never Knows, Do One?; I've Got My Love to Keep Me Warm; If My Heart Could Only Talk; He Ain't Got Rhythm; This Year's Kisses; Why Was I Born?; I Must Have That Man; The

Mood That I'm In; You Showed Me the Way; My Last Affair; and Sentimental and Melancholy. CBS CK-44048.

The Jelly Roll Morton Centennial: His Complete Victor Recordings/This massive five-CD set, with intelligent and lucid liner notes by Bob Greene and James Dapogny, is highly recommended for those who wish to peruse the heart and soul of Morton's craft in fuller detail. It fortunately omits the horrible 1930 recordings he made with the vaudevillian and laughing-clarinet player Wilton Crawley, allowing us to focus on Morton as pianist, arranger, composer, and leader. All known alternate takes are included, which is another plus, and the sound of these transfers is even cleaner and more realistic than on the single CD listed elsewhere. RCA Bluebird 2361-2-RB (five CDs).

Jelly Roll Morton: New Orleans Memories Plus Two/These 1939 piano solos are the last commercial recordings Morton made, and are excellent: Sporting House Rag; Original Rags; The Crave; Mister Joe; The Naked Dance (two tks.); King Porter Stomp; Buddy Bolden Blues; Winin' Boy Blues; Don't You Leave Me Here; Mamie's Blues; and Michigan Water Blues. Commodore/Teldec 8.24062-ZP.

Red Nichols & Miff Mole/This CD duplicates four titles on the Living Era disc but contains twelve more examples of "early cool": Darktown Strutters Ball; Rhythm of the Day; Hurricane; Wabash Blues; Someday, Sweetheart; Davenport Blues; Hot Time in the Old Town Tonight; Delirium; Riverboat Shuffle; Feelin' No Pain; Original Dixieland One-Step; Honolulu Blues; Harlem Twist; Shim-Me-Sha-Wabble; That's A-Plenty; and Corrina Corrine. BBC CD-664.

Djangologie USA, Vols. 1–3, Django Reinhardt/This collection, for those who wish it, completely supersedes the first LP recommended in Chapter 3: I'se A-Muggin'; I Can't Give You Anything But Love; Are You in the Mood?; Oriental Shuffle; After You've Gone; Georgia on My Mind; Limehouse Blues; Nagasaki; Swing Guitars; In the Still of the Night; Shine; Sweet Chorus; Exactly Like You; Charleston; Rose Room; You're Driving Me Crazy; Tears; Solitude; Hot Lips; Body and Soul; Ain't Misbehavin'; When Day Is Done;

Runnin' Wild; Chicago; Liebestraum No. 3; Miss Annabelle Lee; Mystery Pacific; Improvisation; A Little Love, a Little Kiss; In a Sentimental Mood; Parfum; Sheik of Araby; St. Louis Blues; Alabamy Bound; Honeysuckle Rose; Crazy Rhythm; Out of Nowhere; Sweet Georgia Brown; Bugle Call Rag; I Got Rhythm; Sweet Sue; Lady Be Good; Japanese Sandman; Between the Devil and the Deep Blue Sea; Bouncin' Around; Eddie's Blues; and Hangin' Around Boudon. DRG Swing CDSW-8421/23 (DRG, 157 West 57th Street, New York, NY 10019).

Art Tatum: The Complete Capitol Recordings, Vol. 2/This companion volume to the second disc recommended in Chapter 3 includes: My Heart Stood Still; You Took Advantage of Me; I Gotta Right to Sing the Blues; How High the Moon; Makin' Whoopee; Goin' Home; Blue Skies; It's the Talk of the Town; Dancing in the Dark; Tenderly; Just One of Those Things; Indiana; Lover; and Would You Like to Take a Walk? Capitol CDP-92867.

Jack Teagarden: That's a Serious Thing/This disc duplicates five titles from the Living Era/ASV album (I'm Gonna Stomp; Serious Thing; Tailspin Blues; Never Had a Reason; and Fare Thee Well to Harlem) but has the advantage of Teagarden's very first recording (the Kahn version of She's a Great, Great Girl), plus: My Kinda Love; Lookin' Good But Feelin' Bad; Ridin' But Walkin'; You're a Heavenly Thing; Nobody's Sweetheart; Ain't Misbehavin'; I'se A-Muggin'; Blue Lou; The Blues (two tks.); St Louis Blues; St. James Infirmary; Jack-Armstrong Blues; I Cover the Waterfront; and There'll Be Some Changes Made. RCA Bluebird 9986-2-RB.

Fats Waller: You Rascal, You!/A nice companion to the Stash CD: Numb Fumblin'; Ain't Misbehavin'; Honeysuckle Rose; Minor Drag; I'm Crazy 'Bout My Baby; Georgia May; Breakin' the Ice; Baby, Oh! Where Can You Be?; If It Isn't Love; Won't You Get Off It, Please; I Wish I Were Twins; You Rascal, You!; A Porter's Love Song to a Chambermaid; Draggin' My Heart Around; My Fate Is in Your Hands; That's What I Like About You; Harlem Fuss; and Believe It, Beloved. Living Era/ASV CDAJA-5040R.

Bibliography

The following books were used as source references in the preparation of this volume. Those marked with a dagger (†) are recommended for further elucidation on the development of jazz; those with an asterisk (*) are especially pertinent to jazz history.

Berendt, Joachim-Ernst. *Jazz: A Photo History*. New York: Charles Scribner's Sons, 1978.

Berton, Ralph. *Remembering Bix*. New York: Harper & Row, 1974.

*Dance, Stanley. *The World of Duke Ellington*. New York: Charles Scribner's Sons, 1970.

Dixon, Robert, and John Goodrich. *Recording the Blues*. New York: Stein & Day, 1970.

Ellington, Duke. *Music Is My Mistress*. Garden City, NY: Doubleday, 1973.

*Evans, Philip, and Richard Sudhalter. *Bix: Man and Legend*. New Rochelle, NY: Arlington House, 1974.

Henry, Robert. *The Jazz Ensemble*. Englewood Cliffs, NJ: Prentice-Hall, 1981.

†Hodeir, André. *Jazz: Its Evolution and Essence*. New York: Grove Press, 1980.

Kaminsky, Max, and V. E. Hughes. *My Life in Jazz*. New York: Harper & Row, 1963.

Keepnews, Orrin, and Bill Grauer, Jr. *A Pictorial History of Jazz.* New York: Crown, 1971.

*Lomax, Alan. *Mister Jelly Roll.* Berkeley: University of California Press, 1963.

Panassie, Hugues. *Louis Armstrong.* New York: Charles Scribner's Sons, 1971.

Ramsey, Doug. *Jazz Matters.* Norman: University of Oklahoma Press, 1989.

†Reisner, Robert (ed.). *Bird: The Legend of Charlie Parker.* New York: Da Capo Press, 1979.

Rust, Brian, and Rex Harris. *Recorded Jazz: A Critical Guide.* Baltimore: Pelican Books, 1958.

†Schuller, Gunther. *The Swing Era.* New York: Oxford University Press, 1989.

†Shapiro, Nat, and Nat Hentoff. *Hear Me Talkin' to Ya.* New York: Dover Books, 1966.

*Simon, George T. *The Big Bands.* New York: Macmillan, 1967.

Stearns, Marshall. *The Story of Jazz.* New York: Mentor Books, 1958.

Waller, Maurice, and Anthony Calabrese. *Fats Waller.* New York: G. Schirmer, 1979.

Williams, Martin. *Fletcher Henderson.* Notes for Time-Life's three-LP set *The Swing Era: 1936–37*, 1972.

Wilson, John S. *Benny Goodman.* Notes for Time-Life's three-LP set *The Swing Era: 1936–37*, 1972.

Index

The Newmarket Discovering Great Music Series

DISCOVERING GREAT JAZZ: *A New Listener's Guide to the Sounds and Styles of the Top Musicians and Their Recordings on CDs, LPs, and Cassettes*
Stephen Stroff
"This thought-provoking guide covers jazz from its 19th-century jug band beginnings to its bop-revival present, with a glossary of terminology and specific recommendations for best recordings." (*The Washington Post*) Stroff describes eight distinctive periods of jazz history, discusses 125 musicians, identifies the 60 most essential jazz albums and basic jazz library. 208 pages. 30 photographs. Glossary. Reference buying guides. Bibliography. Index.

DISCOVERING GREAT SINGERS OF CLASSIC POP: *A New Listener's Guide to the Sounds and Lives of the Top Performers and Their Recordings, Movies, and Videos*
Roy Hemming & David Hajdu
The lives, sounds, and styles of 52 top crooners and canaries from the 1920s to the present who have influenced the development of pop music and American cultural history are "written about with loving expertise by two writers who can make singers and and their songs live on paper." (Clive Barnes) 320 pages. 38 photographs. Discography. Videography. Bibliography. Index.

DISCOVERING GREAT MUSIC: *A New Listener's Guide to the Top Classical Composers and Their Masterworks on CDs, LPs, and Tapes*
Roy Hemming
Written especially for the non-expert, free of technical jargon, this indispensable sourcebook for buying and listening to classical music from Baroque to New Age covers 60 composers and 150 recording artists performing classical music today. "An excellent guide, Hemming includes so much information that virtually all tastes and preferences are taken into account. It provides invaluable help to the fledgling listener faced with a daunting barrage of pieces and performers." (*ALA Booklist*) 336 pages. Glossary. Index.

Ask for these titles at your local bookstore or order today.

Use this coupon or write to Newmarket Press, 18 East 48th Street, New York, NY 10017; (212) 832-3575.

Please send me:
_____*Discovering Great Jazz*, $10.95, paperback, 1-55704-169-5
_____*Discovering Great Jazz*, $18.95, hardcover, 1-55704-103-2

_____*Discovering Great Singers of Classic Pop*, $14.95, paperback, 1-55704-148-2
_____*Discovering Great Singers of Classic Pop*, $22.95, hardcover, 1-55704-072-9

_____*Discovering Great Music*, $14.95, paperback, 1-55704-115-6
_____*Discovering Great Music*, $21.95, hardcover, 1-55704-027-3

For postage and handling, add $2.00 for the first book, plus $1.00 for each additional book. Allow 4-6 weeks for delivery. Prices and availability subject to change.

I enclose a check or money order payable to Newmarket Press in the amount of $_____.

Name_____

Address_____

City/State/Zip_____

For quotes on quantity purchases, or for a copy of our catalog, please write or phone Newmarket Press, 18 East 48th Street, New York, NY 10017; (212) 832-3575. ss593.pm